Killer Moms

16 Bizarre True Crime Stories of Murderous Moms

By
Jack Rosewood

ISBN: 978-1-64845-063-1

FREE BONUS!

CONTENTS

INTRODUCTION

When most people think of the most notorious crimes and criminals in history, they think of men. The statistics certainly show that men commit more crime in general and also more violent crimes, but women are not without representation. There has been a fair share of notorious female killers throughout history. From Lady Bathory to Lizzy Borden, there is no shortage of femme fatales.

The reasons women kill are usually the same as men—profit, pleasure, and revenge are all motives cited by female killers—although the methods of operation are often slightly different. Women tend to use poison more than men use strangulation and women stab far less than men.

As you read this, you probably don't necessarily find it strange that there have been some pretty notorious female killers throughout history. After all, women have probably been killing as long as men. What makes this book unique is that it chronicles women who have killed their children.

As much as murder is considered the ultimate taboo in our modern society, prolicide—or the killing of one's offspring—is especially loathsome, especially when the killer is the mother. Of course, it is terrible when a father kills his children as well, but a mother develops a special bond with her children after carrying them in her body for nine months.

The breaking of that bond just makes a mother killing her children seem that much worse.

You'll find out, though, as you read through the pages of this book, that the reasons why and the circumstances in which mothers have killed their own are quite varied. Some mothers killed out of jealousy, some due to revenge, and others seem just plain crazy.

You'll read about some high-profile killer moms that you already probably know a little about. Follow along in the Casey Anthony case and decide for yourself if she killed her little daughter. Read about how Andrea Yates murdered all five of her children in cold blood. Remember the Susan Smith case back in the 1990s? That case is also profiled in this book. Although these are all high-profile cases that were heavily covered in the press at the time, you'll read about details that aren't common knowledge and you'll get updates on the current status of these famous killer moms.

They say that revenge is a dish best served cold, but for a couple of these killers moms, they took that aphorism to the next level when they killed their children. The story of Christy Sheats, who was a seemingly normal, average mother, is profiled in this book. As Sheats' marriage was about to fall apart and she believed she was going to lose everything, she killed her children in front of her husband. In a similar type of case, you'll read about South Carolina mother Jessica Edens, who killed her children and then phoned her husband afterward to tell him.

There are a couple of women profiled who killed their children to be with men who didn't want children. Perhaps worst of all are those who killed for profit. Kelly Turner and Diane Staudte are two women who preyed on their children for money and did so in a way that was drawn out and painful.

Finally, a number of these cases defy explanation. Dena Schlosser and Isabel Martinez are two of the most bizarre killers of all, male or female, due to the strange reasons they gave for killing their family members. Both women believe they had a one-way phone line to God and that he told them to kill.

So, strap in for a fascinating and at times disturbing ride. You'll be glued to the pages of this book as you learn about some of the most notorious female killers in American history. Some of these women are serial killers, while others are mass murderers, but they all preyed on their families.

This is truly a collection of 16 of the worst women killers. And they probably don't celebrate Mother's Day.

CHAPTER 1

"I PROMISE YOU WHATEVER YOU WANT," CHRISTY SHEATS

Some people can never let go. Even when they know they've lost their jobs, when they know they've lost an argument, and—often especially—when a relationship is over, there are just some people who will never admit to the cold, hard facts of reality.

Of course, within this subset of people, there is a spectrum. Most just let the loss stew in their minds, holding onto the faint hope that one day they will be able to get back what they lost. On the other end of the spectrum are people who take extreme measures to get back or keep what they believe is rightfully theirs. These people will manipulate, lie, steal, and stalk their object until, usually, it ends badly for them.

And then there are the most intense cases. Those at the extreme of "not letting go" often seem to know that they can never get back what they lost. They rationalize the situation by reacting most irrationally—they take a life or lives.

Often the obsessed take their own lives in a fit of ultimate frustration. The more drastic will take the life of their object and the most disturbed will take the life of their object and several other lives before taking their own. It's a classic case of "If I can't have you, then neither will anyone." It's a difficult thing for most people to contemplate, but unfortunately, it takes place much more than we would like to believe. Most of the cases involve an angry and upset ex-boyfriend or husband, who—often under the influence of drugs and/or alcohol—decides to take his ex's life and anyone nearby along with her.

But occasionally, women are the ones doing the killing in these cases. And that shouldn't be surprising, should it? Women feel those same emotions as men when a relationship ends, especially if they aren't the ones to end it. Women can also obsess over things and sometimes women even get violent. The following is the case of a woman who just wouldn't let go, which resulted in a massacre that rivals any of those committed by men.

On the evening of June 24, 2016, 42-year-old mother Christy Sheats was at her wits' end. Her sanity was crumbling, her marriage was about to end, and she has lost all the respect of her family. So, to punish her husband, Christy did the most desperate thing imaginable—she committed prolicide (or the murder of her children). This is such a noticeable case because the killer mom thought about doing this for some time, planning precisely how she could elicit the greatest effect by the one witness who mattered.

It took less than half an hour, but once the smoke cleared, Christy's and her 45-year-old husband Jason's two daughters—17-year-old Madison and 22-year-old Taylor—were dead and not long after seeing her handiwork, Christy would also be dead at the end of a Katy, Texas cul-de-sac.

Childhood Sweethearts

Christy Sheats was born Christy Byrd in the very average, middle-class, middle American town of Decatur, Alabama. Life is slow and quiet in Decatur, with very little crime. It is a place where neighbors still know and talk to each other. Most people who are from Decatur like it and wouldn't want to live anywhere else because it is such a good place to raise a family.

By all accounts, Christy's life growing up in Decatur was pretty normal and there is no evidence of abuse in the Byrd home; in fact, Christy seems to have been fairly well-adjusted growing up in the 1980s and '90s. She had plenty of friends, dated, took part in school activities, did well in school, and got along with her family.

The truth is that Christy never had any major episode of the type of rebellion that so frequently marks the lives of teenagers. She seemed to be the type of kid any parent would want.

Christy met her future husband Jason Sheats while the two were in high school. They began dating and eventually married. Work brought them to the Houston, Texas area, which is where they decided to start a family.

But it was also where their family tragically ended on that hot June night.

A Rocky Marriage

The first few years of the Sheats' marriage was wedded bliss. They moved into the suburban town of Katy, Texas, and had two daughters, Taylor and Madison. The Sheats family did everything that a middle-class American suburban family does: they went to barbeques and block parties, they went on vacations, and they presented the image of a stable, happy family. Christy was an attractive blonde-haired blue-eyed woman and Jason also had "all-American" looks. They appeared to be the perfect couple.

But the exterior of a happy family was a façade that was slowly falling apart by the late 2000s. The couple began arguing about how the girls were being raised—Jason preferred a more hands-off approach while Christy was a bit of a disciplinarian. Christy wanted to know where the girls were at all times and who they were with, which Jason believed went too far at times. The disagreements turned into verbal arguments,

6

but nothing ever went too far. The disagreements never got physical and the couple always seemed to be able to turn the page.

Or easy-going Jason was able to move on after arguments, at least. Christy, on the other hand, was always a bit obsessive and didn't easily forget about things; she just couldn't let things go. And the bigger the problem, the harder it was for Christy to let go.

Jason and Christy's marriage started to have problems in the 2010s, not due to infidelity or chemical abuse issues but because of Christy's obsessive nature. The couple continued to fight over how their two daughters were raised and Christy became more irrational and combative during those arguments. It got to the point where any mention of the Sheats' daughters triggered Christy's obsessiveness.

Christy was also close to her grandfather. He was the one person who not only listened to all of her problems but also seemed to understand and offer legitimate solutions for all of them. By late 2011, as Christy's mental health began to deteriorate, she came to count on her grandfather's counsel more and more.

But then he died in 2012. The death of her grandfather devastated the already emotionally unstable Christy Sheats. Instead of opening up to her husband and daughters, though, she shut them out and retreated into her world. And it was a dark and twisted world.

As Christy lamented the death of her beloved grandfather, another tragedy struck when her mother died. Although she was closer to her grandfather than her mother, Christy's mom represented the last link to her childhood, which was a happier and more stable time in her life. Christy Sheats retreated once more to her dark world, but this time it would be for good.

As her demons began to collect, Christy decided that she no longer wanted to deal with them or anything else. She attempted to kill herself three times in the early 2010s, resulting in extended mental hospital

7

stays each time. The stress of Christy's deteriorating mental state took its toll on her, but it was just as bad for Jason and the girls.

But the Sheats family learned to deal with Christy's erratic nature and, after a while, even welcomed her extended stays in the psych ward. When she was home, she constantly argued with Jason and the girls about some of the most mundane things, from what they were wearing to where Jason was if he didn't come home immediately after work. The arguments could get pretty heated, so much so that the police were called to the Sheats residence 14 times in 2012 alone!

Jason knew that the situation was bad, but he didn't know how bad it was or if he could fix the situation. After all, she was the mother of his children and he had known her since they were young, so he tried and tried to salvage things.

When Christy received her inheritance from her grandfather, though, Jason began to get a little scared. Christy's grandfather wasn't a wealthy man, so he didn't leave her much, but she did get his prized possession—a .38 caliber pistol. It was a nice gun and well taken care of, but Jason knew it could be a problem and suggested locking it up.

Christy would have none of that! Christy didn't like being told what to do by anyone. Although Christy was politically conservative, she was a modern woman who didn't take well to men, including her husband, telling her how to run her life. She was also a believer in the Second Amendment, so the gun became another source of potential conflict that Jason decided to avoid.

But the gun was the obvious elephant in the room as the familial situation grew worse. Christy applied for a carry permit, but due to her mental health record and the number of times the police were called to the Sheats home, she was denied. It's not easy to get denied for a carry permit in gun-loving Texas.

8

"Just Shoot Yourself"

In the weeks leading up to June 24, Jason was planning on making some important moves. He had talked with some of his family members about divorcing Christy and had researched some area divorce lawyers. The logistics would be settled later, he believed, but the time seemed right to move ahead with the proceedings. He had mentioned divorce to Christy more than once, but the mere mention of the word always seemed to push her near the edge.

On that evening, divorce talk would push her *over* the edge.

June 24 happened to be Jason's birthday, and although he had nothing special planned, he had hoped that Christy wouldn't go into one of her increasingly unstable episodes. Jason attempted to talk to Christy rationally about separating, but she reacted negatively. Later in the day, Christy picked a fight with her oldest daughter about her fiancé, whom she was scheduled to marry only days later on June 27.

As Jason's birthday turned into just another awful but normal day in the Sheats home, frustrated, he told Christy that, "This will be the last birthday you are going to ruin." Little did he know, he was right.

Christy called a family meeting that evening in the living room under the pretense that all four would discuss the numerous family problems. Of course, all of the problems had emanated from Christy, but that mattered little to her because she had decided that her grandpa's .38 was going to do all the talking.

As soon as Christy convened the meeting, she reached into the cushions of the sofa she was sitting on and pulled out grandpa's pistol. She had planned the encounter hours earlier. Thinking that Christy only intended to kill herself, Jason challenged her when he saw the gun.

"Just shoot yourself," he said. "Make it easy on all of us, just shoot yourself!"

9

Christy replied, letting her true intentions be known. "No, that's not what this is about. This is about punishing you!" she said.

And at that point, Christy began opening fire on her two daughters. Jason and his daughters ran for the front door, making it outside, but Madison died on the lawn. Jason managed to call 911 during the attack and could be heard saying, "I promise you whatever you want" to his wife as she closed in to finish her diabolical work.

As Taylor crawled across the front lawn with every little bit of energy she had left, Christy reloaded, went over to her daughter, and fired two more shots. It didn't take the police long to arrive at the quiet cul-de-sac.

When they did, Christy was waiting. She pointed the gun at the officers but was shot in the head and killed with a single shot. It appeared to be a clear case of "suicide by cop." Madison died at the scene from a single gunshot to the neck, while Taylor died later in the hospital from three gunshots to the head.

Jason was uninjured, at least physically speaking. There is no question, though, that Jason Sheats will forever carry the tortured memory of how his wife destroyed his family on his birthday. And, according to Christy's own words and the local law enforcement officers who investigated the case, that was her intent.

"He felt Christy wanted him to suffer," said Fort Bend County Sheriff Tory Nehls. "Christy knew how much he loved Taylor and Madison and how much they loved him." Christy Sheats just couldn't let go of the life she once had and that she probably could never get back. If she couldn't be happy, then neither could anyone else in her life.

CHAPTER 2

THE MADE FOR TV MURDERESS, CASEY ANTHONY

There is no denying that Americans love their crime. At any given time, all you have to do is peruse cable television for a few minutes to find a true crime show or a crime forensics program. If there isn't a true crime show on, then you can probably catch a crime-themed movie on one of your favorite streaming providers.

And if movies and television aren't your things, then there are certainly plenty of true crime books you can pick up at the library, your local bookstore, or on Amazon that will give you your fix of crime. Of course, not just any crime will do. Americans like their true crime stories to be salacious and sometimes a bit gory. Above all, they need to have a good antagonist. Since Americans have traditionally cheered for the underdog, it sometimes helps if the person accused of the crime, or crimes, is good looking, successful, and/or articulate.

It also sometimes helps if the accused is a popular sports star like O.J. Simpson or a former "A list" actor such as Robert Blake. But often a virtual unknown will fit nicely in the role, especially when the supporting players are larger-than-life characters.

This next case fits most of the criteria for being a made for television crime case perfectly. It would be hilarious in many ways—if it didn't revolve around the death of an innocent child. The case in question is the murder of toddler Caylee Anthony by her mother, Casey Anthony.

This case was destined for the ID channel from the start. The antagonist and defendant, Casey Anthony, was a physically attractive yet unsympathetic defendant. Casey looked like an all-American girl, but once details of her lifestyle emerged, the goodwill she initially garnered quickly turned into hate. Quite frankly, for many, she represented some of the worst qualities found in people: greed, vanity, and selfishness. But these are all qualities that work well for television!

The anti-Casey Anthony sentiment was largely driven by the news media that brought the case into living rooms across the United States 24 hours a day, seven days a week. The two networks that primarily covered the case were *Court TV/TruTV* and the *Headline News Network* (HLN), with the latter leading the charge. The most vocal and visible of Casey's detractors was former prosecutor Nancy Grace, who dedicated countless hours on her HLN show to the case.

A case like this also needs at least one colorful lawyer to round out the cast. Anthony's primary defense attorney, Jose Baez, definitely fit the bill. Baez was a somewhat flashy and certainly unconventional lawyer from south Florida who made a living by representing—and often getting not-guilty verdicts for—thieves, murderers, and a host of others who could be in a rogues' gallery. There were also rumors that he and Casey had a bit more than a client-attorney relationship.

But, when all was said and done, the case had to be tried in a courtroom, not on Nancy Grace's television show and not in the court of public opinion. When Casey Anthony was proclaimed not guilty by the jury, it stunned most of the country and made Nancy Grace's and the other professional pundits' heads spin.

Social media reacted quickly to the verdict, which was one of the first cases to extensively involve and be followed by various social media sites. The "Casey Anthony Case," as it became known, became so associated with social media that it was also known as the "Social Media Murder Case."

In the end, the tragic case remains unsolved and unresolved for the most part. Casey is technically free, but the details of her child's death remain shrouded in mystery.

A Wild Child

Casey Anthony was born in Warren, Ohio on March 19, 1986, to George and Cindy Anthony. If you've never been there, Warren is a friendly yet hard-scrabble town just outside the once-thriving industrial city of Youngstown, Ohio. A true union city, the people of Warren were traditionally either employed in one of the area's heavy industries or in supporting sectors. In many ways, Warren was the quintessential "Rust Belt" city.

Warren had begun to change by the early 1980s, though. Much of the heavy industry that the city relied on had left for developing countries. By the time Casey was born, the area's industrial heyday was long past and the population had declined significantly.

But George Anthony was a good provider for his family. George was a police officer who gave his family, which included an older son, Lee, a good life. He eventually moved the family to central Florida so that he and his wife could enjoy their golden years in the sun and his kids would have opportunities he didn't think were available to them in Ohio.

Casey found plenty of opportunities in Florida. Casey never took much interest in sports, academics, or most other extra-curricular activities in high school. Well, the extra-curricular activities that were sanctioned by the school anyway. By the time she entered her teens, Casey began hanging out with other kids who had a similar lack of interest in school functions, so they began cutting class together.

When the school would send absence reports in the mail to the Anthony home or call, Casey would intercept the messages. When they got through, such as at parent-teacher conferences, Casey would show her daddy her big blue eyes and promise to do better.

As is the case with most fathers, George was manipulated by his daughter. But, in a family where both parents are in the home, at least one is usually immune to the wiles of the manipulative child.

Casey, however, was a naturally crafty person and by the age of 16, she had seemingly perfected her manipulative tactics—both of her parents were seemingly under her influence. She knew how to appeal to both of her parents, but that what worked for one often didn't work for the other.

The cutting of an occasional class quickly evolved into skipping entire days and even weeks of class. Casey also began drinking and smoking pot while she was cutting class. Casey and her friends would often rotate partying at their parents' houses during the day when they were cutting class and then sober up enough when they returned home in the afternoon to keep up the pretense that they were still legitimate high school students.

Casey cut so much class that she was unable to walk in her class graduation ceremony, which was a complete surprise to her parents and grandparents who were in attendance. The incident proved to be a major fiasco in the Anthony home and effectively peeled back some of the façades of a sweet girl that Casey had built during her teen years. George and Cindy were no longer convinced that their daughter was so sweet and innocent. But what came next truly eliminated any pretenses that Casey was a "good girl."

Who's Daddy?

While Casey was cutting class with her friends, she wasn't just drinking a little beer and smoking a little pot, she was also having sex. It is no surprise that, when you mix alcohol with hormone-driven boys and a cute girl, things were going to happen. But Casey didn't seem to worry much about consequences.

If there was one common theme that kept surfacing during Casey Anthony's life, it was that consequences were of little concern to her. Birth control wasn't something that she considered and so, as a result, she was pregnant at 19. She wasn't regularly employed, wasn't attending college, and lived at home with her parents. Still, for Casey, life was a party.

Casey hid the pregnancy from her parents for several months. She didn't gain much weight during the pregnancy and she was gone so much from the house anyways that her parents didn't notice. Casey considered abortion but ultimately decided against it and came clean with the news to her parents. Needless to say, they weren't happy.

George and Cindy were supporting Casey financially and they knew that, unless their daughter's behavior and attitude changed very quickly, that they'd be looking after their future grandchild as well. Still, they decided to support their daughter through the pregnancy and to see what would happen. They had to find out who the father was, but that turned into an adventure in itself.

When Caylee was born in 2005, Casey had a supposedly steady boyfriend named Jesse Grund. Jesse thought that he was Casey's only boyfriend at the time and he also thought that Caylee was his child. He wasn't prepared for fatherhood, but he did his best, and by all accounts, he was doing better than Casey. He spent time with Caylee, and unlike Casey, he had steady employment.

But then the DNA test came back. Jesse wasn't Caylee's father! To this day, it isn't known who Caylee's father is. It was later revealed that the father could have been any number of men, and the number was quite significant. To Casey, though, the identity of her child's father didn't seem very important. Not much of anything seemed very important to Casey Anthony, except partying and being the center of attention.

And she wasn't going to let a little thing like motherhood get in the way of her good time. When Caylee was still an infant, Casey looked into giving her up for adoption. In a rare instance of self-awareness (although it was the result of selfishness), Casey told her family that she wasn't a good mother and that she was considering giving Caylee up for adoption. In retrospect, it would've been the best decision for all parties involved, but Cindy Anthony's grandmotherly impulses took hold.

Cindy told Casey that she would help raise Caylee and that they could live at the family home as long as they needed it. She also told her that she and George would help financially as long as she made an effort. It was a good deal for Casey as it allowed her to continue her lifestyle unimpeded. Casey thought she could do and go virtually wherever she wanted and her parents would be there to watch Caylee, just like on-call babysitters.

In return, the Anthonys required—or more like requested—that Casey make some positive changes in her life. She was supposed to find regular employment and make a more serious attempt at being a mother. Casey agreed, but the effort she made was minimal at best.

The Disappearance

Casey and Caylee officially lived at the Anthony home but were gone quite a bit. Casey continued her hard-partying ways, occasionally worked, and sometimes stayed with friends or her latest fling. Needless to say, it wasn't the most stable situation for Caylee.

The Anthonys tried to do what they could to provide a good home for Caylee, but conflicts with Casey were constant. She didn't want to be told to grow up and didn't appreciate being compared to her older, more responsible brother.

On June 16, 2008, things came to a head in the Anthony home. Casey and Caylee were at the Anthony home for most of that day. They used the pool and Casey used the family's computer while her parents spent time with Caylee. But just as happened so many other times, an argument broke about between Casey and her parents. George and Cindy wanted to know if Casey was working, and if not, if she was looking for full-time employment. They also wanted to know where she and their granddaughter were staying when they weren't at the family home. Casey didn't want to hear any of it. Casey took Caylee from the home and George and Cindy didn't hear from their daughter for a month.

George and Cindy didn't bother trying to contact Casey for the first couple of days. They knew their daughter could be emotional and volatile and that it was sometimes best to let her cool down and come to them. When she didn't call them, though, they started to worry a little, especially about Caylee. They knew that Casey wasn't a very responsible mother and that she had a tendency to forget, or not care, about doing basic things for her daughter.

After a couple of weeks, Casey finally called Cindy and told her that she and Caylee were doing well. She told her mother that they were staying at a friend's home and that the reason she didn't return their calls was that she was busy looking for work.

Cindy was skeptical and asked questions, especially about Caylee's status, but Casey had an answer for everything. Casey said that she had landed a good job at Universal Studios and that Caylee was staying with a nanny named Zenaida Fernandez-Gonzalez, "Zanny," while she worked.

Cindy was glad to hear from Casey and that everything seemed to be going well, but she was suspicious because things seemed to be going *too* well for her normally unambitious and troubled daughter. And the story about the mysterious nanny named Zanny was strange, to say the least.

But there was nothing Cindy could do. Cindy knew that, if she kept pushing Casey, then Casey would push back and it might be several more weeks before she could see her granddaughter. So the Anthonys waited.

Then, on July 14, George and Cindy were notified that Casey's car had been in an impound lot since June 30. George and Cindy picked the car up on July 15 and immediately noticed that it had been parked for a few weeks. Casey had not been taking care of the car, but when George opened the trunk to clean it out, he was taken aback. There was a smell. He had smelled it before when he was a police officer. It was the smell of death.

George and Cindy were able to get in contact with Casey, who came to the Anthony home without Caylee. Casey continued to tell the story that Caylee was with Zanny, but the story changed slightly, with Zanny now a potential kidnapper.

More worried about Caylee than Casey was, Cindy called 911. "I can't find my granddaughter," Cindy Anthony said to the 911 operator. "She [Casey Anthony] just admitted to me that she's been trying to find her by herself. There is something wrong. I found my daughter's car today and it smells like there's been a dead body in the damn car."

The 911 operator then asked to speak with Casey. "Can you tell me what's going on a little bit?" asked the operator.
"My daughter has been missing for the last 31 days," Casey replied.
The 911 Operator then asked, "And, you know who has her?
"I know who has her," answered Casey. "Her name is Zenaida Fernandez-Gonzalez."

According to Casey Anthony, her daughter was kidnapped by a nanny named Zanny, for some unknown reason, at a time that wasn't clearly defined. It was the beginning of a series of lies that would continue to grow and grow.

A Mountain of Lies

George and Cindy were distraught that their granddaughter had been allegedly kidnapped by her nanny, but when they asked Casey why the woman would do such a thing, she couldn't give them a logical answer. At times, she implied that maybe Zanny wanted Caylee for herself, while at other times, she suggested that it was part of an elaborate international kidnapping scheme.

The Orange County Sheriff's Department took the lead in the case, supported by the Orlando Police Department because the supposed kidnapping took place in that city. Almost immediately, things didn't seem right to the investigators. The "Zanny" story seemed off to all of the investigators involved. Seasoned detectives know a lie when they hear one and they can often tell when a person is lying. When a story changes as much as it did with the Zanny story, the person telling it is usually lying.

Then there was the matter of Casey's demeanor. She didn't seem very upset about the situation and when the Anthony family organized search efforts, Casey was nowhere to be found.

Well, she was somewhere to found: it just wasn't searching for her missing daughter. It turns out that after Caylee had supposedly been kidnapped by Zanny, Casey was partying at one of the area's best-known nightclubs—Fusion. Photos emerged of Casey dancing seductively with men and women on the floor of the nightclub and it was learned that she even took part in a "hot body" contest one night.

To her friends and acquaintances, Casey was more upset that she didn't win the hot body contest than the fact that her daughter was missing. This was the pattern for the entire month between the time when Casey and Caylee left the Anthony home on June 16 until the police were called on July 15. Casey simply went on with her life as if nothing had happened and as if she never even had a child. She went to other bars and nightclubs besides Fusion, went to dinner with her friends, and spent time with one of her boyfriends, Tony Lazzaro.

Lazzaro later said about that month, "She was the way she was every day—happy. Happy to see me. Having a grand old time." Casey also never told Lazzaro that Caylee was missing, and when the police asked him about Zanny, it was all new information to him. Frankly, it was new information to everyone who knew Casey and Caylee. None of Casey's friends and family had heard about the mysterious Latina nanny before, never mind had met the woman.

So, detectives with the Orange County Sheriff's Department decided to dig a little deeper into the identity of Zenaida Fernandez-Gonzalez. It turned out that there was a woman named Zenaida Fernandez-Gonzalez who lived in the Orlando area, which shouldn't be all that surprising considering that Florida has considerable Cuban, Puerto Rican, and other Latin American communities. With that said, the detectives were able to conclusively determine that the Zenaida Fernandez-Gonzalez who was living in the Orlando area at the time had no connection whatsoever to Casey or Caylee Anthony.

Anthony later claimed that she had met a woman with that name more than a year earlier, but that she had made up everything else about her being Caylee's nanny. The investigators believe that the woman was made up and the name came from Casey's love of the prescription drug Xanax.

The realization that Casey made "Zanny" up had some serious implications. First, it meant that Casey would lie to her friends, family, and police about something deadly serious. Second, the lie certainly suggested that she was hiding something. The detectives still had to determine what it was that she was hiding, but it was something to do with Caylee.

Either Casey knew what had happened to Caylee or she was involved directly in some way. Any good detective knows that, once you catch a "person of interest" in a crime in a lie, then that person immediately becomes a suspect. All good detectives also know that is the time to put on the heat.

During their interrogation of Casey, the detectives decided to press her on another issue—her supposed job at Universal Studios. The detectives had already done their background check and learned that Casey wasn't actively employed anywhere, so when she told them that she worked at Universal, they asked her what department she worked in and who her boss was. When Casey's answers proved to be as fluid as a bottle of her cheap perfume, they offered to drive her down there to refresh her memory.

When they arrived at Universal Studios, Casey finally admitted that she didn't work there. Casey Anthony had always been able to manipulate things to her advantage through a combination of her good looks and an ability to lie. It wasn't that she was necessarily a good liar though; just that she was willing to lie. You see, most people rarely lie, and when they do, they often feel guilty about it and either get caught or just admit that they lied.

For Casey Anthony, lying was second nature, but she met her match with the Orange County detectives. Not only did Casey's lies make her look guilty in the eyes of the police, but they were also criminally prosecutable. On July 16, 2008, Casey Anthony was arrested for child endangerment and interfering in a police investigation. She was given a hefty bond of $500,000, and after the local news reported on the case, it slowly made its way up the food chain to the cable networks.

The case took its first high-profile turn when Casey was bailed out of jail. She had no money of her own to make bail and neither did any of her lovers, or they were unwilling to do so. George and Cindy Anthony didn't post the bond either.

Curiously, the bond was posted by a high-profile California bounty hunter named Leonard Padilla. Padilla is best known for dressing like a cowboy and going after big-name criminals. One of the biggest cases he was involved with was the Speed Freak Killers serial killer case during the mid-2000s in northern California. In that case, he worked with one of the killers to locate victims' bodies so their families could have closure.

So why did Padilla use his own money to bail Casey Anthony out of jail? Padilla later said that he believed Casey either knew what happened to Caylee or she had something to do directly with her death. He claimed that he only wanted to find the girl's body and to get some resolution on the case. After bailing Casey Anthony out of jail, Padilla met with her to discuss the impending case.

He not only didn't get the information he sought, but he left the meeting with a completely negative view of Anthony. Padilla went on Nancy Grace's television show shortly after meeting with Casey Anthony, saying that the young mother was a promiscuous narcissist. Not exactly a ringing endorsement from your bail bondsman!

What Casey did next showed either a lack of intelligence, a lack of self-awareness, or a little of both. While out on bail, she was arrested on August 29 for writing checks stolen from one of her friends. It was certainly not a good look for Casey, who was by that time the subject of daily television shows, newspaper articles, and blog entries. Casey Anthony and the disappearance of Caylee was quickly becoming the hottest story in America.

As friends and family of the Anthonys held out hope that Caylee was still alive, the detectives working the case knew that she was probably dead. They hoped that, while Casey was cooling her heels in the can for passing bad checks, they could gather more evidence and build a case against her. And the circumstantial evidence was starting to pile up.

But George and Cindy had not given up on their daughter. No matter what she had said, or possibly even done, they still loved her and wanted to believe that she had nothing to do with Caylee's disappearance. They posted the $500,000 bond and brought Casey home.

Charges Without a Body

Casey's homecoming was far from joyous. According to reports of those close to the Anthony family, the tension between Casey and her parents could be cut with a knife. Although George and Cindy still wanted to believe that Casey didn't kill Caylee, they were starting to believe that she knew more than she was saying.

The detectives also believed that Casey knew more than she was letting on; they thought she had something to do with the little girl's death. But what evidence was there that Caylee was dead?

While Casey was going in and out of jail, the detectives were busy putting together the evidence needed to charge her with more serious crimes. The evidence of human decomposition in the trunk of her car was certainly damning, as were her general behavior and some internet searches she possibly made from the Anthony home. But all of that was circumstantial evidence, and even with all that combined, it would be difficult to prove in court that Casey was the killer of her child.

And there is little doubt that it would be extremely difficult to get a conviction without a body. Although a body is not needed in Florida to prove murder, it is more difficult to do so without one.

So, all of these factors made getting a murder conviction against Casey Anthony an extremely difficult proposition, but the Orange County prosecutor decided to move ahead with the case anyway by charging her with murder on October 14, 2008. No doubt the prosecutor's office felt pressured by public opinion, which was being driven by intense media coverage. So Casey was jailed, charged with first-degree murder, and refused bail.

Casey Anthony was facing a potential death penalty, and in Florida, death penalties are routinely carried out. As Casey served her sentence in the county jail, a major development in the case began taking place near her family's home.

Roy Kronk was a meter reader for the local utility company. While working as a meter reader for several years, he had been chased by dogs and unhinged homeowners and had seen some pretty strange things. He had, for the most part, learned to look past most of the strange things he saw and just do his job, but something in a wooded area near the Anthony home didn't look right. He was aware of the case, so he phoned the police.

The first time Kronk called the police, he was forwarded to a tip line, which is where his tip disappeared. He called the police twice more in August to tell them about what looked like a plastic bag next to a skull in the wooded area. The police searched the wooded area after the third call and found nothing. It makes one wonder what they were doing.

Finally, on December 11, 2008, Kronk called the police a fourth and final time. The cops were a little more thorough during that search, finding the remains of a child inside a plastic bag. DNA tests later revealed that it was Caylee Anthony. The prosecutors had their body and the apparent proof that Caylee Anthony was murdered. They just had to prove the killer was Casey.

A Media Circus

The national media began hovering around the Anthony home as soon as some of the details about the case emerged. Once Casey was charged with her daughter's murder, surveillance of the Anthony home became a non-stop part of the news cycle.

Many of the more "law and order" pundits on cable television dedicated almost all their time to trashing Casey Anthony. Not that any help was needed in that respect, but Geraldo Rivera, John Walsh of *America's Most Wanted* fame, and former prosecutor turned talk show pundit Nancy Grace, all spent ample time making the case against Anthony.

Of course, it was all about the ratings, which went up for all of the pundits. For Nancy Grace, who had essentially been a "B-list" anchor on *Court TV* before the case, it proved to be a professional boon as her audience increased by more than 150%.

Gavel to gavel coverage of the proceedings was provided by *Tru TV* (formerly *Court TV*), and if you missed any of the live coverage, replays were available late at night, or you could get recaps from Grace or one of the other pundits.

Of course, there was also the internet. The Casey Anthony murder case is often cited as one of the first "social media murder cases," partially because of some of the evidence in the trial, but primarily because Facebook, Twitter, and various blogs drove the news cycle. The Baby Boomers were still the primary consumers of news media in 2008/09, and they preferred traditional media such as television, newspapers, and magazines, but Gen Xers and Millennials had less use for Nancy Grace, Geraldo, and John Walsh. When all types of media coverage of the case were considered together, it truly was the trial of the century.

Not a Slam Dunk Case

By early 2011, the pre-trial motions were all done and the lawyers had assembled their teams. Linda Burdick led the prosecution for Orange County while Jose Baez fronted the defense team. As Casey Anthony didn't have the funds to pay for such a high-profile attorney, Baez took the case *pro bono*—well, sort of *pro bono*. And Jose Baez was certainly one of Florida's most high-profile lawyers.

Baez came from somewhat humble beginnings, earning a law degree a bit later in life as he worked to put himself through school. He eventually built a nice criminal defense practice in Florida, often successfully defending people charged with murders and other major felonies. Baez took Anthony's case under the assumption that she would pay later, although many have questioned that unique form of payment since nothing about Casey Anthony's life before the murder trial suggested that she would ever be able to pay any sizable amount of money.

Some suggested that Baez had an affair with Anthony, although that is little more than a rumor. Others have pointed out that Baez is a shrewd businessman as well as a lawyer and that defending such a high profile client only helped his brand. After all, in the social media trial that was the Casey Anthony case, making your name known could pay major dividends.

The trial finally began on May 11, 2011. The prosecution's case was, for the most part, circumstantial, but it was substantial none the less. A strand of hair found in Casey's car was consistent with Caylee's and showed signs of a process known as "root-branding." Root-branding only takes place after death, which means that Caylee was deceased when she was in her mother's car.

Then there was the decomposition in the trunk. Not only did the trunk give off the scent of death when it was recovered from the impound lot, a cadaver dog "hit" on it. Of course, Caylee's body being discovered only about a quarter of a mile from the Anthony home was also another piece of circumstantial evidence against Casey.

Then there were the Google searches. A search of the Anthonys' home computer revealed that someone had been doing some pretty "interesting" research. The phrases "neck breaking" and "how to make chloroform," among other macabre phrases, were entered numerous times, with chloroform-related searches being entered more than 84 times.

The prosecution's case was simple: Casey Anthony suffocated Caylee in cold blood because she no longer wanted to be a mother. Other evidence was also used that showed Casey frolicking and having a good time before and after Caylee went missing.

The defense surely had their work cut out for them, but Baez was up to the task. He only needed to cause doubt in the minds of the jury, and if he could do that, then there was a chance Casey would walk free. The other option was that she could be found guilty of the lesser charge of manslaughter and possibly get time served or serve very little time in state prison.

So, Baez decided to use a strategy of reduced culpability. He argued that Caylee died in an accidental drowning and that Casey was guilty of being negligent and possibly a bad parent, but in no way guilty of first-degree murder.

Baez skillfully tiptoed around some of Casey's more egregious lies but placed the blame on George Anthony for the disposal of Caylee's body. He claimed that Casey only listened to her father because she was afraid of him after years of sexual and physical abuse. Needless to say, the abuse claims proved to be the final bridge that was burned between Casey and the rest of her family.

The Verdict and Aftermath

After nearly two months of testimony, the case went to the jury. To the pundits and most of America, the verdict seemed like a foregone conclusion. Surely they would find her guilty of murder, most people thought. After all, Casey didn't do herself any favors when she appeared to laugh at one point when a medical examiner was describing the wounds to her daughter. But the jury saw things differently to most of America.

On July 5, 2011, the jury announced that they had found Casey Anthony not guilty of first-degree murder, manslaughter, and felony child abuse but guilty of misdemeanors relating to her lying to the police. She was sentenced to time served and ordered to pay $4,000 in fines. Most importantly, Casey Anthony was free to go anywhere in America, or the world, for that matter.

The reactions to the verdict were swift and intense. Nancy Grace and most of the other media pundits were shocked—at least they acted as such—and all but said the jurors were dumb. For their part, most of the jurors have avoided media attention since the trial, but those who have been brave enough to give interviews have said that they simply didn't believe there was enough evidence to convict.

The presiding judge, Belvin Perry, also tried to avoid most of the media scrutiny but did offer an interesting opinion on what he believed happened. "The most logical thing that happened was that she tried to knock her daughter out by the use of chloroform and gave her too much of chloroform, which caused her daughter to die," said Perry. Why Casey felt the need to "knock her daughter out," though, has never been established.

Several politicians across the United States also felt the need to get involved by proposing "Caylee's Law" in some states. The different versions of Caylee's Law make it a felony to *not* report a missing child to the police. Many questioned if it said more about our society that such a law needed to be passed or that it took so long to do so.

For the Anthony family, the aftermath has been devastating. Casey is now estranged from her entire family, who are left picking up the pieces of Caylee's death and the harm that was done to their otherwise good reputations. Although few people believed the accusations Baez made toward George and Lee Anthony, some did. Losing her family honestly didn't mean much to Casey, other than having lost a stable place to stay.

Casey did have to go into hiding due to numerous and credible death threats after the trial. She decided to stay in Florida and is said to be in a relationship and living with a man named Patrick McKenna, who was one of the private investigators on her defense team. Casey has filed for bankruptcy due to the enormous cost incurred by the trial. Baez has reportedly billed her more than $300,000, the Orange County Sheriff's Department another $200,000, and private company Eqisearch sent her a $400,000 bill.

Anthony has given few interviews since the trial and has been difficult to locate, but in a 2017 interview, she gave a very illuminating answer when asked what she thinks about her image. "I don't give a shit about what anybody thinks of me," said Anthony. "I don't care about that. I never will. I'm OK with myself. I sleep pretty good at night."

CHAPTER 3

KELLY TURNER AND THE MAKE A WISH MURDER

One of the unfortunate realities of the world we live in is that there are a lot of people out there who don't want to work for a living. These people would rather have others work for them, victimize others for money, or both. Most of these types of people can be ignored, as long as you don't get caught up in one of their schemes, but that becomes more difficult when children are involved. Those who use children for their scams are certainly the worst of all criminals.

Unfortunately, this is a situation that happens much too frequently around the world. Some parents have been known to teach their children how to beg, lie, and steal money. There are also plenty of cases where parents use their children to defraud the government for government benefits. These are certainly cases of child abuse, but even in those cases, as twisted as they are, the parents in question usually have some love for their children. They may not be thinking of the long-term consequences of their actions and how it will affect their kids, but in their minds, they are committing those crimes at least partly for them.

But then there are the rare cases where the parent sees their children as little more than a golden goose that can be disposed of once they are done. Or worse still, they learn that the act of disposing of their child can net them some more money. This is what happened in the case of Colorado mother Kelly Turner.

Kelly Turner was a young, single mother who, in 2015, announced on social media that her 5-year-old daughter Olivia was suffering from a host of potentially terminal illnesses. The heart-wrenching posts Kelly made on her social media accounts and GoFundMe page resulted in good-intentioned people giving her more than $22,000. Kelly then got more than another $500,000 worth of medical care from Medicaid for her daughter.

But things never added up with Kelly. When the Colorado authorities began asking questions in 2017, Oliva suddenly succumbed to her illnesses. Or did she?

In what can only be described as one of the cruelest twists to one of the most heart-wrenching cases of a child's death, it looks like everything was a big scam perpetrated by Kelly Turner. Oliva was sick, and unfortunately, she did die, but it now looks like her mother planned her long and painful death just for some money and sympathy.

Kelly Renee Turner

Kelly Renee Gant was born in 1978 in the Houston, Texas area. At this point, she is a bit of a mystery other than she was potentially raised in an abusive household. She grew up in the Houston area, but little more is known about her early life. She married and had a daughter and then Olivia was born in 2010, but the marriage didn't last.

Based on a combination of statements from those who knew her, and from the current court proceedings, there are a few things that are known about Kelly Turner. Kelly was the kind of person who could blend into a crowd and disappear. She was not particularly attractive, nor smart or engaging, and she never seemed to have a job. But she was friendly and seemed to be a good mother to her daughters. She had a reasonable network of friends in Texas, although she never seemed to be close to her family. Some of her friends noticed her lack of relationship with her family but didn't think too much about it because such relationships are more common today.

Things were not easy for Kelly and her daughters. Since Kelly never worked, she had to rely on her girls' father and the state of Texas for her relatively meager living expenses. On top of her financial problems, Kelly told her friends that Olivia had been diagnosed with a plethora of medical issues in 2013. And then, as quickly as Kelly told her friends about Olivia's problems, she decided they were moving to the Denver, Colorado area.

"I questioned her moving to Denver because Houston has a world-renowned children's hospital," friend Ruby King said. "Why would you live somewhere else?"

Yes, it did seem like a very strange move for a woman in Kelly's situation to make. Besides the superior medical facilities that Houston had, Kelly also had a support network in Texas, and Olivia had her friends. But Colorado has better government benefits.

It now appears that Kelly Turner moved to Colorado solely to scam the federal government, the state of Colorado, and the good people of Colorado out of their money. Kelly had no intention of working in Colorado, but she had a ready-made cash machine in the form of her "sick" daughter. The fact that no one knew her in Colorado made her long-term plans all the more achievable.

She began by defrauding Medicaid in 2014 by making false claims about Olivia's health. Sometimes, she did bring Olivia to doctors, apparently to establish a degree of legitimacy to her claims. The doctors also diagnosed Olivia with a host of illnesses, which meant that checks would be sent to Kelly. But since Kelly was just trying to get money, once the diagnoses were made and the government agreed to pay, she quit bringing Olivia in for treatment. By early 2015, Kelly had developed a very intricate backstory for her daughter's illness.

Neuro gastrointestinal Encephalomyopathy

Mitochondrial neuro gastrointestinal encephalomyopathy syndrome, often shortened to neuro gastrointestinal encephalomyopathy is a rare disease that affects the ability of those with it to digest food properly. The disease can be quite painful, and even when treated, it can lead to death. It often begins in the digestive system, but it can evolve and attack many of the body's vital organs.

In early 2015, Kelly began telling her friends and family in person and on social media that Oliva was afflicted with this rare disease and that she needed their prayers and support—and most importantly, their money!

Kelly Turner may not be the smartest woman, but she is savvy and is fully aware of trends. When she began her long-term scam of using her child to defraud government agencies and private individuals, she knew that the internet and social media were the keys to make the big bucks.

The first thing Kelly did was set up a blog called "Prayers for Olivia Gant" in 2015. The website gave updates on Olivia's "condition," showed pictures of her and Kelly, and allowed friends, family, and strangers to leave messages and words of support. The blog also listed contact information detailing how those truly concerned could donate money. Finally, and most importantly, the blog directed those interested to Olivia's GoFundMe page.

In recent years, GoFundMe has become a popular way for people to raise money for a variety of different things. The website is extremely user-friendly; within a matter of minutes, a person can put a page up soliciting donations from every corner of the globe. Pictures and extra text are optional, but in the case of Olivia's account, Kelly made sure to post plenty of pictures of the cute little girl.

In the text on the page, it stated: "We are hoping for support both financially, spiritually, and emotionally. Not only will this be a taxing time for Kelly (mom), and Olivia but for Olivia's sisters and the friends and family who are willing to step in and help during this time."

And plenty of people were willing to step in and step up to help Olivia and her mother. The account eventually went above $20,000, which allowed Kelly to move with her daughters into a better apartment. Most didn't think much of the move since better living conditions were certainly something a terminally ill child would need. But then a lightbulb, albeit a very dim one, went off in Kelly Turner's head.

She reasoned that since Olivia's supposed illness got them plenty of cash, maybe it could also garner them some fame and attention. Most people who are in the middle of committing such an egregious crime try to avoid attention, but Kelly Turner seemed to crave it more the deeper she got into her scam.

Kelly went to the Denver area Make a Wish Foundation, which found Olivia's story credible and heartbreaking. Olivia's wishes were relatively down to earth and fairly inexpensive. She went on a few ride-along evenings with the local police and was given a Batgirl themed party by the Make a Wish Foundation. Local news cameras were there to document most of the events, with Olivia seeming genuinely happy. Kelly was there every time as well, sometimes stealing much of her daughter's thunder as the reporters tried to ask questions. This was Kelly's time to shine, and if her daughter had to die in the process, then so be it!

Olivia Loses Her Battle

By the summer of 2017, Olivia's condition had severely deteriorated. None of the medications and treatments Olivia was given seemed to work. She was constantly sick and in pain, so her doctors advised that she be placed in a hospice where she could be given around-the-clock-care. Olivia Gant finally lost her battle against her mother in August 2017.

The doctors at Children's Hospital Colorado who had cared for Olivia and were familiar with her case were immediately suspicious. It seemed strange that Kelly had quit bringing Olivia in for treatments after the government agreed to pay. The disease that Kelly claimed she had was never definitively diagnosed and the precise cause of her death remained unknown. The doctors knew that she had been suffering for some time and her little body just gave out, but they couldn't say for sure what killed her.

Then Olivia's older sister became ill. The bizarre turn of events made the doctors look more closely at the entire situation and prompted them to call Colorado human services. Social workers determined that there was certainly smoke and that everything should be investigated, so the local police were also called.

Homicide detectives, who are a naturally cynical lot, also thought things didn't add up. Since the death certificate said Olivia died of various illnesses and not homicide, however, there was little they could do. At least for the time being.

The detectives knew that something awful had happened to Olivia though, so they kept the case open and kept pushing the district attorney's office to search for other avenues of investigation. Finally, in 2018, after a year of investigation, a judge signed off on warrant that allowed for Olivia's body to be exhumed by the district attorney. Another autopsy was done that was more thorough, revealing that the little girl's cause of death was quite different than what her mother claimed.

The autopsy showed that Olivia had not received medical care for some time before her death and that she was malnourished. Although the autopsy couldn't precisely say what killed Olivia, it appeared to have been the result of a prolonged lack of care. Most importantly, the autopsy proved that Olivia showed no signs of the many diseases that her mother said she had.

The news of the new autopsy spread rapidly through Denver by word of mouth and the local news media, and eventually, nationwide via social media. People were angry and felt betrayed. "How could a mother victimize her child for profit?" was the common question. It was the question that everyone wanted to be answered and it could only be answered by Kelly Turner or in a courtroom.

Munchausen Syndrome by Proxy?

Kelly Turner was charged with the first-degree murder of Olivia Gant in October 2019 and is currently awaiting trial in the Douglass County, Colorado jail. The local community breathed a sigh of relief when Kelly was arrested and the police were praised for staying with the case.

"I am extremely proud and impressed with the determination of all agencies involved, especially my detectives. While it has been an extremely emotional case, they have investigated all aspects of it with diligence and professionalism," said Douglass County Sheriff Tony Spurlock.

Although the case has yet to go to trial, based on the evidence uncovered so far, it looks like Kelly Turner will be spending a considerable time—probably the rest of her life—behind bars. As Turner winds her way through the legal system, everyone in Colorado is hoping that she will answer the question everyone is asking: why?

There was clearly at least a profit motive for Olivia's murder. Kelly never worked and didn't seem interested in ever having a legitimate job, and as her defrauding of the Medicare demonstrates, she also knew how to pull a con for profit.

But many people familiar with the case don't think that explains everything. They argue that Kelly could have pulled numerous financial cons without having to kill her daughter, never mind killing her in such a slow, agonizing manner. Some experts believe that Kelly Turner displays all the signs of Munchausen syndrome by proxy.

Munchausen syndrome is a clinically recognized disorder whereby the afflicted person feigns symptoms of a disease to gain attention. Those who commit the disease by proxy pick another person, usually a child or a vulnerable adult, to be the recipient of the feigned symptoms. Some close to the case think Kelly may have this syndrome because there is possible evidence that she was the victim of it in her childhood.

Other people close to the case are not convinced, believing instead that Kelly Turner is nothing more than a cruel con-artist who used her child to make a few bucks and get some attention, before heartlessly disposing of her. The case will probably go to trial in late 2020, but if public sentiment is any indication, things don't look good for Kelly Turner.

CHAPTER 4

SERIAL KILLING HER KIDS, MEGAN HUNTSMAN

Serial murder has a decidedly masculine appearance. Male serial killers get the most media attention by far, as they are the subject of most serial killer documentaries and fictional serial killer movies. Statistically speaking, the reputation is well-deserved, with men making up about 90% of all serial killers throughout history.

But with 10% remaining, that still means that women make up a considerable minority of serial killers. So why don't we hear more about female serial killers?

Part of the reason may be that female serial killers usually don't fit the ready-made media mold of how society sees serial killers. Male serial killers are known to "hunt" their victims and often do so for pleasure and lust. A number of the better-known male serial killers—Ted Bundy, Jeffrey Dahmer, the BTK Killer—raped and tortured their victims as part of an elaborate yet sick and twisted ritual.

Outside of Aileen Wuornos, who gunned down seven men in the late 1980s and early 1990s, few female serial killers hunt down their victims and even fewer appear to be driven by a sexual sadist impulse. Female serial killers also tend to kill those closest to them.

One of the more common types of female serial killers throughout history has been the so-called "black widows." These are women who kill their husbands and partners, usually for financial gain but also sometimes seemingly for the thrill of the kill. The most commonly used weapon by black widows is poison, ranging from sedatives and tranquilizers to ethylene glycol (antifreeze). One of the more famous black widows of recent history is Canadian Melissa Ann Shepard, who may have murdered three of her husbands during the 1990s and 2000s. We'll get to a notorious antifreeze black widow later in this book.

The so-called "angels of death" is another type of common serial killer, although this type is not necessarily specific to just women. These types of killers murder those they are entrusted to watch, claiming their victims in hospitals, nursing homes, and private homes. Many of these killers are professional nurses, such as Kristen Gilbert, who killed four people in her care in Massachusetts hospitals during the 1990s.

The case of Megan Huntsman has some similarities to black widow and angel of death cases, but in other ways, it is truly unique in a most twisted way. Like an angel of death, Huntsman killed six of her children who were under her care, but like a black widow, she did so to get them out of her life. But unlike a black widow, who usually kills for financial motive, Huntsman killed so she could do methamphetamines.

Megan Huntsman may not have gained pleasure from the act of murder itself, but there is no question that she killed to gain pleasure. She was driven by drug addiction and the feeling it gave her. She was so driven by that addiction that she killed six of her newborn children to keep using drugs.

A Lack of Confidence

Megan Huntsman was born in 1975 to a middle-class family in suburban Salt Lake City, Utah. By her early teens, Megan had grown into her looks and turned out to be an attractive, petite brunette, but according to her mother Joyce, she lacked confidence.

Megan was an average student, and although she got along fine with her teachers and classmates, she didn't have many friends. But one friend she did have was Darren West.

West was also a loner who had a bit of a wild side. He liked to party and often drank alcohol and smoked marijuana while in high school. Megan was definitely attracted to the bad boy loner, but he also treated Megan well and seemed to have the potential to be a good provider, so when he proposed to her, she readily accepted. Megan was married at age 18 and pregnant with her first child shortly thereafter.

Although Megan and Darren were a young and inexperienced couple, by all accounts, they were good parents to the two daughters they had in the early 1990s. By the middle of the decade, though, things began to slowly unravel.

Darren and Megan always liked to party a little by drinking, but after a few years of marriage, the drinking became problematic. The couple often fought in front of their children while they were drunk. At other times, either or both of them would be gone for days at a time on drinking binges. But binge drinking was nothing comparing to binge tweaking.

Not So Pleasant Grove, Utah

The couple eventually moved into a home owned by Darren's family in Pleasant Grove, Utah. Darren's family hoped that the home would bring some stability to the increasingly chaotic familial situation, particularly for the children. No one from either the West or Huntsman families knew just how far Darren and Megan had descended into addiction, nor would anyone have imagined just how depraved Megan would become.

The couple had become heavy methamphetamine users by the mid-1990s, with neither working a legitimate job. Their daughters were afterthoughts in their lives, which became almost exclusively focused on getting high and getting more meth to get high.

The two developed hundreds of dollars per day habits, which were supported by Darren selling and manufacturing meth. Darren's activities kept a constant flow of meth coming into their Pleasant Grove home, but he was also gone a lot, so he didn't see just how bad things were getting.

Megan's looks went quickly. Her skin wrinkled and aged and she began losing her teeth, yet she still kept snorting and later smoking more and more meth. Megan's and Darren's descent into drug addiction didn't stop them from having sex or from Megan getting pregnant at least eight times from the late 1990s until 2006. The pregnancies were a problem for Megan because they put a serious crimp on her meth use.

Megan Huntsman wasn't going to let anyone or anything get in the way of her glass meth pipe. By all accounts, Megan was able to keep the majority of her pregnancies a secret from her family, friends, and even Darren, so she and he claim. Due to her heavy meth use, Megan usually didn't put on much weight during her pregnancies and when she did, it usually wasn't much and she was able to claim that it was normal weight gain. When labor came, she simply went into the garage and gave birth.

What came next was truly horrifying. Megan would cut the umbilical cord that connected her to her newborn child and coldly put her thumb on the baby's throat, snuffing its life out in a matter of minutes. She also wrapped a hair tie around her victim's throat at least once.

Not only were Megan's victims the definition of the word vulnerable, due to Megan's extreme drug use, but they were also in extremely poor health when they were born. After claiming a victim, Megan would put the child in a box or other type of small container, almost like a coffin, and tuck her away in a corner of the garage. At this point, it is difficult to say if she was keeping the bodies as a twisted memorial or if she preserved them as a memento, similar to other more "traditional" serial killers.

In the middle of her killing spree, Huntsman had to let one of her children live in 2000. She later said that the only reason why she let her daughter live was that she started to show her pregnancy more than usual, and therefore, it would have been impossible to cover up the crime. This proves that, despite being in a decade-long meth-induced delirium, Megan Huntsman still knew right from wrong. And she premeditated the murder of all her infant children.

The situation in the West household took another turn when Darren was arrested on federal drug charges in 2006. A DEA operation in Utah caught Darren in its net of mid-level dealers and manufacturers. After being charged with a very lengthy and very serious list of crimes, Darren pled guilty to possessing chemicals intended to manufacture meth. He was sentenced to 12 years in federal prison.

Megan's life took some drastic turns while her husband was in prison. Without her reliable and constant stream of meth, Megan's use of the drug tapered, although it didn't end altogether. She did the drug when she could, but alcohol became her drug of choice after 2006.

The couple also divorced while Darren was in prison. Long prison sentences so often do end relationships and the separation that the two experienced made them realize that, despite having three daughters together, they were probably better off apart. They seemed to thrive on each other's negative energies and fed each other's addictions.

Megan quit having children and seemed to settle down, but after the divorce, she was asked to leave the family home in Pleasant Grove. Darren's family still owned the home and didn't want his ex-wife, whom they blamed for a lot of his problems, to keep living in the home on their dime. So Megan moved out into a trailer park in the nearby town of West Valley City, Utah.

When Darren West was released from prison in early 2014, he returned to the home he once shared with Megan Huntsman and their three daughters. He still had contact with his wife because their youngest daughter was still a minor, but he was trying to avoid her for the most part. In April 2014, he decided to clean the house up, intending to clear out all of the bad memories of his meth-fueled past. When he got to the garage, he found more than he could have imagined.

Hidden behind several medium-sized boxes, West found a small box covered with electrical tape. He never remembered putting the curious-looking box there, but much of the late '90s and early 2000s were a drug-induced blur.

He cut the tape with a pocketknife, opened the box, and was horrified to find what looked like the remains of a human infant. He immediately called the local police.

Detectives from the Pleasant Grove Police Department arrived at the West home within an hour and began their investigation. They were, of course, skeptical of West and looked at him as a potential suspect, but the fact that he called and allowed them to search the home had made him look less guilty.

After an exhaustive search of the home, the police found the bodies of seven more infants hidden in small boxes. Lab tests later revealed that one of the infants was stillborn but the others were suffocated. The police needed to talk to Megan Huntsman.

Megan wasn't difficult to locate and she also was quite willing to talk. She seemed relieved when the police asked her about the infant bodies that were stashed around her former garage. Megan Huntsman admitted to everything, but the worst part is that she didn't even know how much destruction she had caused.

Huntsman confessed to killing all but one of her babies, stating that she did so because she couldn't feed any more mouths while she was feeding her meth addiction. The one that she didn't kill was stillborn, no doubt a result of Huntsman's meth addiction. With that said, Huntsman could offer few details to the police about the actual murders, other than to say that she suffocated her babies.

Her mind was so clouded from meth by 2014, though, that she didn't even know how many of her babies she had killed. She guessed it was eight or nine, but she wasn't quite sure. Megan *was* sure that her husband wasn't involved.

It may be hard to believe that her husband wasn't involved in any of the murders or that he didn't even know his wife was pregnant, but it must be remembered that he too spent over ten years in a meth-induced fog. For those reasons, and because he was the person who called the police, Darren West has never charged in connection with the murders of his six infant children.

Guilty Plea

Although Megan Huntsman confessed to the police, she pled not guilty to first-degree murder charges. Of course, this was more legal maneuvering than anything. Utah has the death penalty, and in a conservative state with high birthrates, there's a good chance that just about any jury would not only find Huntsman guilty but also sentence her to death.

So, she went through the motions of the hearings, but in April 2015, about one year after she was arrested, Huntsman decided to plead guilty to all six counts of first-degree murder, as long as the prosecution took the death penalty off the table.

The judge handed Megan six sentences of five years to life in prison. Three of the sentences are to be served consecutively, which means that Huntsman must serve 49 years minimum behind bars before she is eligible for parole. Huntsman was 40 when she was sentenced, so she will be 89 before she is even *considered* for release.

"I don't think she'll ever be released," said prosecuting attorney Jeff

Buhman in a later interview. But Megan Huntsman will have a life behind bars, sort of. She will be allowed certain privileges, such as visits from family if she stays out of trouble. And as terrible as her crimes were, Huntsman still has the backing of some of her family members.

Megan's mother still supports her, placing much of the blame on drug addiction and Darren West. Most importantly, Huntsman's two oldest daughters still support her and plan to visit her in prison.

For the people of the usually quiet state of Utah, Megan Huntsman's crime is impossible to fathom. The god-fearing, conservative people of the state can't understand how a mother could kill her child, never mind go on a serial killer spree on her children.

Utah governor Gary Herbert perhaps best summed up the attitude of his state's people. "We can't wrap our minds around it or draw any kind of rational conclusion to why," he noted in an interview. "It's just such a tragedy. I suspect there are mental health issues there we don't know about. It just makes me sad."

CHAPTER 5

THE COLD AS ICE MOM, MICHELLE BLAIR

You have to be a tough person to live in some of America's inner cities, especially Detroit, Michigan. Detroit consistently ranks at the top of all of the most negative indexes—poverty, crime, and murder rates are among the highest in the United States, and in some categories, is comparable to many cities in developing countries—making it one of the least desirable places in the country in which to live.

Turnered, there are many good people in Detroit, but the thieves, gang members, drug dealers, and killers make the city a living hell for many people. Unfortunately, Detroit has many "cold" people who have no regard for human life.

One of Detroit's coldest inhabitants is a criminal who killed two people in 2012. This criminal didn't murder rival criminals or even random people for a few dollars—this criminal's victims were her children.

The cold-blooded killer in question is a middle-aged woman named Michelle Blair, who took out her lifelong anger and hate on those she was supposed to love and protect—her 13-year-old daughter and her 9-year-old son. Once she had killed her children, Blair demonstrated just how cold she was by storing their bodies in a freezer.

Blair later claimed that her younger, surviving son was being sexually abused by his siblings, which is why she killed them. The police didn't take long to determine that her story was not only a lie but that it also covered up far greater abuse that was taking place in Michelle Blair's home.

Detroit is truly a tough city and the homicide investigators who worked on the Michelle Blair case had already seen their fair share of gruesome murders, but when they pulled the bodies of Stoni and Stephen from the freezer, even the most seasoned investigators were sick to their stomachs.

But the discovery of the bodies in the freezer was only the tip of the iceberg. The investigators learned that Michelle Blair was a woman who had no business having a single child, let alone four children. She had an extremely short temper, which she routinely took out on her helpless children. For Stoni and Stephen Blair, living with their mother was one long torture session that was full of never-ending pain and misery. They had nowhere to turn and no one would help, not even other members of their extended family.

A Life of Poverty, Crime, and Abuse

There's no doubt that Michelle Blair had a tough life as a child in Detroit. She grew up in an unstable home with plenty of crime and poverty all around. She was raised by a single mother who didn't give her much guidance and reportedly failed to protect her, as Michelle was said to have been sexually abused as a child.

Blair learned a much tougher version of life than what most people receive. She learned that crime and "hustles" were the quickest way to "get over" in life and that having sex was no big deal and could be used as a tool to get what you wanted. Michelle became sexually active as a teenager and quickly became a single mother.

By the late 2000s, Michelle Blair had four children with two different men, neither of whom paid any child support. Both of Blair's children's fathers were career criminals and were constantly in jail or prison, which is part of the reason why they failed to financially support their children; but there is no indication that they would have made any effort anyway because they rarely came around for visits when they weren't incarcerated.

Blair was no angel herself. She had numerous run-ins with the law, although most of the charges were minor and nothing that prevented her from getting public assistance. Michelle Blair never showed much maternal instinct toward her children but stayed off birth control because the more children she had, the more money she received from the government.

Government assistance would quickly become a way of life for Michele Blair. In America, receiving government aid doesn't mean you can't work,. Many state and federal aid programs are set up to help recipients with job training and they are generally encouraged to find work. Aid isn't intended to be permanent, so besides the carrots of the incentives, there are several sticks used, such as agencies only paying for a portion of a recipient's rent.

Despite receiving aid for rent, Michelle Blair usually had problems coming up with the minimum amounts because she had problems keeping down part-time jobs. It would be an understatement to say that Michelle Blair's life was a hot mess.

Michelle Blair may have been born into some unfortunate conditions, but she did nothing constructive with her life to change. She made no steps to learn any job skills, such as vocational training, and she never took the time to learn about money management or other basic life skills. So what did Michelle Blair do with her time, if she wasn't working, going to school, or doing anything of value?

The evidence shows that she spent most of her free time abusing and torturing her children. Her oldest child, who was 17 in 2015, told investigators that she and her younger siblings were routinely hit and whipped with extension cords, sticks, and tree branches, often colloquially known as "switches," and were burned with hot irons. According to Blair's daughter, the slightest thing could set her off. If the kids were fighting, Blair might single one out for a beating or burn him or her with a curling iron. If Michelle was having relationship problems, or if her government check wasn't as big as she had hoped, then one of her kids usually had to pay.

The torture continued for several years, partly due to two reasons: the children didn't attend school, and Michelle's extended family didn't seem to care. Somehow Michelle got away with claiming her children were "homeschooled," although there are no official records of them taking any tests or passing any grades. Needless to say, Michelle Blair was the furthest thing from a professional educator, so she certainly wasn't teaching her children anything of value.

Still, somehow Blair got away with the charade of "homeschooling" her children without coming to the attention of the authorities. Blair's extended family was also of no help to the children. According to Blair's oldest child, family members knew about the regular beatings but didn't think they were that bad and never said anything, so the abuse continued. But, in 2002, someone did report Michelle Blair to Michigan social services.

A social worker visited the Blair home, took a look around, and filed a report. In 2005, social services received another complaint about Michelle Blair, so a social worker was dispatched to the Blair home once more. As with the first visit, the social worker found nothing out of order, so the report was filed but no further action was taken.

It remains unknown who filed the abuse complaints against Blair. Since the abuse was so bad in the home, it really could've been anyone: a family member, a neighbor, a food delivery person, or even a meter reader.

The Murders

Michelle Blair and her few supporters later claimed a variety of reasons for the murders, essentially saying that they were not planned nor premeditated. Although it is probably true that Blair didn't plan to kill her children the way a serial killer sets out to kill person after person, she put both of the children she killed through immensely painful torture sessions that any normal person knows could only end in death.

Nine-year-old Stephen was the first to die. Stephen could never seem to do anything right in Blair's eyes. Whenever the kids were fighting, as kids that age so often do, Stephen was blamed for it. If Stephen's younger brother did something wrong, Stephen was blamed for it. Anything bad that happened in the family's townhouse was blamed on Stephen.

When Blair abused Stephen, she particularly liked to choke the helpless boy. She would often choke him with a belt, almost to the point of suffocation, before loosening it and letting him go. She also liked to wrap plastic bags around his head, cutting off the air supply until he was on the brink of unconsciousness. Blair would then revive Stephen and berate him before sending him on his way.

Blair also liked to torture her son with hot water. If Blair perceived Stephen as being out of line or if she just was feeling cruel—which could pretty much be on any day at any time—she would fill up a bathtub with scalding hot water and make Stephen soak his feet in it until they blistered.

Blair also thought it was fun to surprise her son while he was taking showers by throwing boiling water on him. The torture of Stephen continued throughout 2012, but it got much worse during the summer. Michelle thought of new and crueler ways to abuse her son, such as by making him drink Windex and other household cleaning products.

Finally, on August 30, 2012, Michelle Blair took one of her torture sessions too far. The reason why she wrapped a plastic bag around his head one last time isn't quite clear and it doesn't matter. Stephen was probably just too weak after being abused so much and he couldn't fight his mother anymore. Or maybe he just finally gave up.

What is known is that, on that day, Blair suffocated Stephen and he didn't wake back up as he had done every other time. As Michelle Blair looked at the lifeless body of her son laying on the living room floor, she surely knew she had a problem. There was no way she could explain this to child protective services or the local police, so her criminal instincts kicked in—she had to cover up the crime.

Michelle Blair was never and will never be accused of being very bright and she was also never known to be very ambitious, so how she attempted to cover up her crime reflected her personality in many ways. She simply wrapped Stephen's lifeless body in a blanket and then put him in a large freezer in the house. Michelle Blair was as cold as ice.

The other Blair children knew about the murder, but they knew better than to say anything to the authorities or anyone else for that matter. Each of them knew that they could be their mother's next victim, so they decided to keep their mouths shut. The Blair children learned how to keep their abuse within the walls of the home, although in the long-run it never really helped them. With Stephen dead, Michelle turned her rage on Stoni.

Michelle Blair didn't need an excuse to abuse any of her children. However, she did seem to have at least one kid for whom she saved her worst abuse. In the months after Stephen's murder, Blair began dishing out much of the same torture and abuse to Stoni. Then, nine months after her younger brother was murdered, Stoni made the mistake of saying she didn't like her surviving siblings.

In any other familial situation, it would have been a rather innocuous statement. Kids say things like that all the time about their siblings, and there was no doubt that she was still grieving over the death of her younger brother. Stoni was probably confused and angry about the entire situation and missed her brother. She was also probably scared the same thing could happen to her. And for good reason. Blair didn't want to hear it from Stoni though and she didn't want to hear *anything* about Stephen.

She had killed Stephen and supposedly erased his name from the memory of the family and now she was going to do the same to Stoni. Michelle grabbed a t-shirt that was laying on the unkept floor of the home and choked Stoni with it. She had choked Stoni several times before, but as happened with Stephen, this time she had gone too far and choked the life out of the teenager.

Since Stoni was 13, she was a little bigger than Stephen, so Blair needed some help disposing of her body. For this macabre task, she enlisted the help of her oldest child, who was 15 at the time. Blair's oldest child didn't even think of refusing her mother at this point. They put Stoni in the freezer with Stephen and Blair went on about her life. No social workers, police, or even extended family members asked about Stephen or Stoni. It was if the two kids just disappeared off the face of the Earth and no one cared.

The Eviction

For the most part, life went on as normal for Michelle Blair in the two years after she killed Stephen and Stoni. She abused her surviving children but was careful not to take things too far and no one asked any questions. Social services weren't called again and Blair kept collecting her government money.

The bodies of Stephen and Stoni sat in the freezer and would have remained there if Blair had done the most basic things. Her income was almost entirely from government aid and the government paid for most of her rent through the Section Eight program, but she was required to come up with a small portion every month.

But since Blair couldn't seem to hold down even the easiest part-time jobs, she wasn't able to meet the minimum payment criteria of Section Eight. And if you don't pay your rent, even if you're in the Section Eight program, you'll eventually get evicted.

But it wasn't like the eviction would have come as a surprise to Blair. She was given numerous warnings by her landlord and the eviction process was entirely by the book, which meant she was given court dates and finally given notice that the sheriff's department would come to evict her. For whatever reason, Blair decided to wait in the townhouse and let the process play out. Or maybe she didn't think they would evict her because she was a single mother. Either way, she was in for a surprise when sheriff's department deputies showed up with an eviction crew on March 24, 2015.

Surprisingly, the crew later said that Blair seemed remarkably calm when they began hauling her possessions to the curb. Chairs, dressers, and electronic equipment were all brought to the curb before the crew finally got to a large freezer. They unplugged the freezer and opened it up to empty it, but were stopped cold in their tracks by what they found.

They were horrified to find the bodies of two children in the freezer frozen stiff. The deputies on the scene had seen a lot of mayhem and murder on the streets of Wayne County, but this was the first time they had seen something like this.

Michelle Blair was promptly arrested and brought into the police station for questioning. Most importantly, her children were sent into county protective services where they got their first good night's sleep in their lives.

The homicide detectives who questioned Blair were disturbed and confused about the entire situation. They wanted not only to know why Michelle had killed two of her children but also why she thought that putting them on ice for two years was a good idea. The case seemed so preposterous and surreal on so many different levels.

For her part, Michelle Blair didn't deny that she had killed her children, but she offered numerous and often conflicting stories to mitigate her guilt. She was promptly charged with two counts of first-degree murder and booked into the Wayne County jail with no bond.

The local Detroit media made Blair's case their top priority, not just because of the heinous nature of the crimes, but also because of the defendant's numerous outbursts in court. Blair would scream and yell at the judge, prosecutors, the cameras, and even her attorneys. If she was thinking about taking the case to trial, her behavior in the courtroom alone would have been enough for a conviction.

Blair's lawyers suggested she plead guilty to one count of first-degree murder, which she did in July 2015 at the age of 36. The guilty plea gave Michelle Blair one last chance to show Detroit and America just how dysfunctional she was. For most criminal defendants, the guilty plea allocution is a chance to show contrition and to hopefully get some leniency from the courts.

For Michelle Blair, her guilty plea was a chance to show the world just how cold she was by giving the court a metaphorical middle finger. Instead of saying she was sorry and asking for forgiveness, Blair blamed her children's fathers for not supporting her more and even blamed the victims for sexually abusing her youngest child. "As horrendous as everyone thinks I am, that's fine. But I'm the only one not lying about anything," said Blair at her sentencing. The investigators found nothing that could substantiate the abuse claims. The judge was not impressed with Blair, to say the least. He sentenced her to life in prison.

Michelle Blair is now where she belongs in more ways than one. She most certainly belongs in prison for the rest of her life to keep the rest of her children safe, as well as others in Detroit, but she also deserves to be there as punishment for her cold-blooded crimes. Prison so far seems to be the perfect fit for Blair. She has spent most of her time in segregation, as she doesn't get along with her fellow inmates or guards. Blair has been assaulted by other inmates, and in turn, she has assaulted other inmates and even thrown urine on guards.

The female inmates and guards of the Michigan Department of Corrections may have to contend with Michelle Blair for decades to come, but at least the people of Detroit are finally rid of her.

CHAPTER 6

THE FEMALE "FUGITIVE," DIANE DOWNS

There's a good chance you've seen the hit 1960s American television show *The Fugitive* at some point in your life. Or maybe you caught the 1993 film of the same name that was a remake of the series. If you haven't, both the series and film are about a doctor named Richard Kimble who was unjustly convicted and sentenced to death for the brutal murder of his wife.

The twist was that the real killer was a "one-armed man."

In the series and the film, Kimble escaped from custody on his way to death row and embarked on an odyssey where he helped numerous people in need on his way to finding the real killer. The show was a huge success and had an impact on the Baby Boomer generation in America, which possibly includes our next killer mom.

On the evening of May 19, 1983, emergency room nurses and doctors at the small hospital in Springfield, Oregon were startled when a young woman came running into their ER. She was hysterical and appeared to be injured, possibly by a firearm.

She told the doctors and nurses that she and her three children had been shot as they were parked on the side of the road. One of the children later died and the other two were seriously wounded. The children's mother, who was 27-seven-year-old Diane Downs, had also suffered a gunshot through her left arm. The scene was as bizarre as it was horrific. It was not something that usually took place around Springfield, especially since it appeared to be a random attack.

When the local police came to the hospital to question Downs about the attack, things quickly took an even more bizarre turn. Diane told the police officers that she and her children just happened to be parked alongside a quiet country road at night when a mysterious "bushy-haired" man walked up to the car and opened fire.

The police took note of everything and put out an all-points bulletin with the description of the assailant, but things just didn't add up. Downs' story was just too tight as if she had taken it from a Hollywood script. It almost seemed like a plot from a 1970s "B" exploitation film—a drug-crazed hippy wandered until he came across some unsuspecting family to victimize

As strange as this case began, and as much as the "bushy-haired man" may have brought to mind the "one-armed man," this case got even stranger as it continued. Diane Downs eventually went on trial for the murder and attempted murder of her children, but she proclaimed her innocence throughout, and just like the fictional Richard Kimble, she even escaped from prison. Unlike the fictional Richard Kimble though, Diane Downs was not a likable person.

Diane Frederickson

Diane Downs was born Diane Frederickson in 1955 in Phoenix, Arizona to a middle-class family. Frederickson was born into a much more conservative America and Arizona was one of the most conservative states at the time. It was the home state of Barry Goldwater, which was a sign of Arizonans' conservative political and religious beliefs.

And the Fredericksons fit right into that mold. Diane's parents were church-going, Bible-toting people who raised their children to be the same. By all outward appearances, Diane was also a god-fearing Christian girl, but it all turned out to be a façade. She hung around the wild kids in the neighborhood and experimented with alcohol, drugs, and sex. After all, it was the late 1960s, and despite its conservative underpinnings, Phoenix had a considerable counterculture scene.

It was a situation where two cultures and generations were clashing and Diane Frederickson was right in the middle of it all. Her friends from school were on one side, while her parents and family were on the other. For a time, Diane tried to straddle both sides of the precarious cultural line.

Diane went to a small Bible college in California after she graduated from high school, but she was expelled after less than a semester for having sex with young men on the campus. The news was a shock to the Frederickson family and scandalous among their Christian friends and family. They felt betrayed by Diane, not just for what she had done to get expelled, but by the fact that she had presented herself in an entirely different way to them. Diane was clearly showing sociopathic signs at a young age.

The expulsion created a rift between Diane and her parents that was never fixed. She left home at age 17 and drifted for a while before meeting Steve Downs in 1973. The match wasn't necessarily made in heaven—far from it—but it provided both people with something they wanted yet was lacking in their lives. For Diane, it gave her a sense of stability and protection that she had lost after becoming estranged from her parents. She had a roof over her head and knew when and where her next meal was.

For Steve Downs, Diane was a real catch, or so he thought. She was young, attractive, and willing to give Steve children. After having a low-key wedding, the couple decided to set up house in the Phoenix area. Diane gave birth to daughter Christie in 1974, Cheryl Lynn in 1976, and son Stephen Daniel "Danny" in 1979. Stephen got the children he wanted, but he also got much more than he bargained for in the marriage.

Steve and Diane constantly fought over many of the normal things that couples argue about, such as finances and how to raise the children, but the major obstacle in their relationship was infidelity. Diane had never really left her wild ways behind her and although Steve thought that marriage would tame her, he found out otherwise.

The marriage problems were aggravated after Danny was born, primarily because Steve didn't think Danny was his child. Finally, in 1980, after years of conflict, the two decided to divorce. Diane would have primary custody of the couple's two—I mean three—children and Steve would pay support.

Once the divorce was finalized, Steve paid support and visited his children, but Diane didn't seem to care much if he was around. She had her sights set on someone else. Steve had good reason to believe that Danny wasn't his son. Their marriage hadn't stopped Diane's wild ways, and while the couple was married, she was known to have more than one paramour. After they divorced, Diane set her sights on a guy at her work.

Diane worked for the United States Postal Service in Phoenix for most of the 1970s, which is where she met fellow postal employee Steven Knickerbocker. Knickerbocker was a young, handsome man who was working his way up in the postal hierarchy. He seemed like the perfect guy for Diane, especially after her divorce was finalized.

Knickerbocker certainly liked Downs, at least physically, and even briefly considered a more permanent, long-term relationship with her. But there were two major barriers to Knickerbocker and Downs staying together for the long-term.

First, Knickerbocker was married. By the early 1980s, divorce rates in America were peaking, so getting a divorce would not have brought the sort of shame it did even ten years earlier. It did still bring about problems. Spousal support could have been a problem, not to mention costly divorce proceedings. And, as exhilarating as his relationship was with Diane, Knickerbocker knew that his wife was more stable, reliable, and trustworthy.

Second, Knickerbocker was not a fan of children. He and his wife had no children of their own and if he were to marry or even cohabitate with Downs then he would essentially become an instant stepfather. Fatherhood was not something Steven Knickerbocker had ever considered or wanted.

So, Knickerbocker broke things off with Downs and went back to his wife. When Diane pressed him, he told her that he didn't want children. Emotionally devastated, Diane Downs decided to move her family as far away from Phoenix as possible.

The Bushy-Haired Man

Getting spurned by Knickerbocker proved to be a major turning point in Diane Downs' life and the lives of her children. She decided to move far away from Phoenix, so she took a job as a mail carrier in Springfield, Oregon. Springfield is located next to Eugene in the scenic Willamette Valley. The area is an outdoor lover's paradise, with plenty of hiking, camping, fishing, and hunting opportunities.

But Diane Downs didn't move to Oregon to enjoy the beautiful vistas; she moved there to escape her past. Diane worked every day and by all accounts was a good worker, yet she never really connected with any of her fellow employees. She always seemed distant and distracted—she had something major on her mind.

Of course, that something major was Steven Knickerbocker. She just couldn't get over Knickerbocker and move on past the relationship. Diane tried contacting Knickerbocker by phone, but he never returned her calls. She then sent him scores of letters, but they were always marked "return to sender."

In Diane Downs' mind, the one thing keeping her from being with Steven Knickerbocker—actually three things—was her children. "This was a real obstacle as far as Diane was concerned, those kids were a burden, and there was no way, that she could see, she was going to get this guy up to Oregon as long as she had the kids," said Lane County, Oregon detective Doug Welch about Diane Downs' apparent conundrum.

Diane had a killer solution to her problem. Downs' supposedly brilliant idea involved murdering her children to get sympathy from the public, and ultimately, win back Knickerbocker. There was just one problem with Downs' plan—all of it.

Diane Downs was truly a narcissist, which gave her the mindset to even think that doing such a thing was okay, but she wasn't a criminal. She just didn't think like a criminal and never considered how her crimes would be viewed by the police and the public. Diane thought that, after the deed was done, she just had to shed a few tears, and then her boyfriend would run to her.

On the night of the attack, Diane told her children that they were taking a little trip and then she loaded them into the car. She then drove outside of town a couple of miles to a fairly isolated area, got out of the car, walked around to the passenger side, and pulled out her .22 caliber pistol.

It happened so quickly that her children didn't have a chance to react. She put several rounds in each child and shot herself once to make it look good. Cheryl died at the scene while her two siblings were hanging on for dear life when they arrived at the emergency room.

Downs was stitched up quickly but held at the hospital. The police had a few questions for her. "From the beginning it was wrong," said detective Welch. "Here was a woman who was completely apathetic about the welfare of her kids."

But any cop will tell you that everyone grieves differently and people exhibit a wide range of reactions and emotions during a tragic situation. The more the detectives investigated the case, though, the more it looked like Downs was lying to them.

She told the police that a mysterious "bushy-haired" man attacked them, but nothing appeared to have been stolen and there was no sexual assault or even an attempted sexual assault on Diane or any of the children.

The alleged perpetrator could have been a random serial killer—the Pacific Northwest had had its fair share of them during that era—but the chances of that were extremely low. Not to mention that a seasoned killer would probably have been more efficient, either by using a higher caliber weapon or by bringing enough ammunition to finish the job.

No, to the homicide investigators, it looked like an amateur job done by someone with little to no criminal background.

The crime scene also revealed some interesting information. There was no gunpowder residue in the car, which meant that the shooter fired from outside the car. Diane claimed that the mysterious bushy-haired man reached into the car and began shooting. Most telling was that there was no blood on the driver's side.

Diane also couldn't seem to tell the police a consistent story. Her description of the alleged shooter changed several times, as did how he shot her and the children and how many shots he fired. She also claimed to have driven to the emergency room at a high speed, but witnesses saw her driving down the street at about ten miles per hour. One witness claimed that the only reason why he noticed her was that she was driving so slowly.

The police theorized that she drove so slow in the hope that her children would bleed to death. Still, the police had no hard evidence. Forensic science was still a few years away from DNA profiling and there were no witnesses who saw the crime. The county prosecutor knew that it would be tough to convince a jury that a mother tried to kill her children for a man, so they continued to gather evidence.

They conducted a couple of searches of Diane's home that gathered some more evidence, and finally, in early 1984, the prosecutor believed it had enough to make a case. Diane Downs was arrested on February 28, 1984 on one count of first-degree murder and two counts of attempted first-degree murder.

She was facing either life in prison or the death penalty in the state of Oregon.

A Circumstantial Case

The case against Diane Downs was strong, but it was far from airtight or a "slam dunk." All of the evidence was for the most part circumstantial, although it was certainly a lot of circumstantial evidence, and when considered as a whole, it was quite damning.

Besides the evidence already mentioned, Steve Downs testified against his former wife. Steve told the jury how his wife was unfaithful, not a very good mother, and was obsessed with Steven Knickerbocker. Knickerbocker was also called to testify by the prosecution, stating that he broke off the relationship because he didn't want children. About the only physical evidence were some .22 caliber shell casings found in Diane's home that matched those from the crime scene. It didn't matter that the murder weapon wasn't recovered because the casings linked Downs—or someone in her home—to the shootings.

Perhaps the most damning and heart-wrenching evidence presented against Diane Downs was the testimony of her daughter Christie. Christie testified that Diane loaded her and her siblings into the car, pulled over on the lonely road, and began opening fire on them. She said that her brother Danny was sleeping but that she was awake and remembered mostly everything.

63

Christie Downs was a very believable witness. The verdict was announced on June 17, 1984—guilty on all counts! No one was surprised by the verdict, although Diane shed some crocodile tears and flailed around a bit. At that point, though, most people could see through Diane Downs' little charade and knew that she was only upset that she had been found guilty and would more than likely spend the rest of her life behind bars.

Diane Downs was sentenced to life in prison plus 50 years, which meant that she had to do a minimum of 25 years behind bars before the parole board would even consider releasing her. Downs was quickly whisked away and sent to the state women's prison in Salem.

The people of the Willamette Valley hoped it would be the last time they would hear from Diane Downs.

The Female Fugitive

Diane Downs entered the women's prison as a high-profile inmate with a target on her back. Although women's prisons tend to be a little different than men's prisons, and far less dangerous, they do have some of the same pitfalls.

Many of Downs' fellow prisoners were mothers, and although they may have not been the best mothers, most of them weren't too keen on a woman who attempted to murder her three children for a man. Still, many of the female prisoners blamed men for their situations and knew that men could often influence their women to do some pretty awful things.

So, Diane navigated the prison carefully. She kept a low-profile and tried to get along with all of the guards and inmates. She took part in whatever activities she could to get a little more freedom and began looking for a way out.

First, she filed appeals, but those were denied. Downs probably never really thought she would win on appeal, but there was always a chance. She also talked to anyone willing to listen about her case. Diane kept blaming the mysterious "bushy-haired man" for the attack and claimed that like the fictional Richard Kimble, she would one day capture the true killer.

On July 11, 1987, she would have her chance. The details of how the events came about are still unknown, but what is known is that, on that day, Diane Downs decided to give herself parole more than two decades early. Diane had several advantages that allowed her to escape. First, she had blended in effectively with the inmate population during her three years in prison. The guards never really paid much attention to her, so when she made her break for the razor wire fence, she did not have watchful eyes on her.

Second, she had the advantage of being in a less secure facility. The women's prison in Salem was far less secure than most of the men's facilities in Oregon at the time and it was also less secure than many women's prisons in other states. Still, she had to crawl through some razor wire and past a guard tower to get to freedom, and once she did, she was on the streets of the state capital.

Downs' freedom didn't last long, though, as she was recaptured ten days later. And unlike Kimble, she never caught her "bushy-haired man." The officials of the Oregon Department of Corrections determined that Diane Downs was too much of a security risk after her escape. They made a deal with the state of New Jersey to house her in their maximum-security prison for women, and years later, they made a deal with the state of California, which is where she is currently being held.

Aftermath

Diane Downs' violent, selfish act on the evening of May 19, 1983, devastated her family and sent shock waves throughout Oregon that continue to reverberate today. The immediate and most obvious victims were her three children who were in the car that night. For whatever reasons, Steve Downs didn't take custody of Christie or Danny after the shootings. Since he never thought Danny was his child, this is somewhat understandable, but he also didn't take Christie with him back down to Arizona. Instead, the lead prosecutor in Diane's case adopted both Christie and Danny. The two changed their names and were raised in anonymity, in a loving, stable household.

In still yet another twist to this case, it turns out that Diane Downs had got pregnant before she was arrested. It was not a responsible move on her part, but what could you expect from a woman who tried to murder her three children and then blame it on a mysterious "bushy-haired man," right?

Downs' fourth child was taken from her when she went to prison. The baby girl was adopted by a family, and like her two siblings, was raised by a loving family in anonymity. When the girl reached adulthood, she appeared on an episode of *Oprah* to discuss her most unconventional upbringing.

As for Diane Downs? Well, she's been cooling her heels in the California Department of Corrections but is eligible for parole from time to time under Oregon state law. She first came up before a parole board in 2008 and was quickly denied before being denied again in 2010. Downs will be eligible for parole again in 2021 when she will be 65.

Most people familiar with the case don't give Downs much of a chance of getting parole in 2021 or at any point, for that matter. Parole is given to inmates who meet two criteria: they must show that they are rehabilitated and are no longer a threat to the community, and they must also show a level of contrition. For Diane Downs, the first point is questionable, although thankfully she no longer has any children around her to kill.

The second point is what will probably keep her in prison, though.

Downs continues to deny that she had anything to do with the attack on her children. Instead she blames the mysterious "bushy-haired man" and even expanding her story to include law enforcement conspiracies. She has a lot of time to come up with bizarre stories.

Diane Downs' own words hurt her in the past and they continue to be a major reason why she probably will never be released from prison. In an interview she gave while awaiting trial for the attack on her children, she gave a bizarre and cold answer to a question about how she feels about their loss. "And they give me love, they give me satisfaction, they give me stability, they give me a reason to live and a reason to be happy, and that's gone, they took it from me, but children are so easy to conceive," she said. Her attitude has changed little since then.

CHAPTER 7

THE SERIAL KILLER WHO WAS RELEASED, MARYBETH TINNING

Serial killers are rarely ever released from prison, and in the United States, this is even rarer. Sure, by law in many states, serial killers who are serving life sentences have the opportunity—the right—to appear before a parole board. Often these parole hearings are a formality and sometimes they are a spectacle: do you remember Charles Manson? But sometimes a known serial killer is released from prison.

One of the best known and most recent such case in the U.S. was Loren Herzog. Along with Wesley Shermantine, Loren Herzog was one half of the "Speed Freak Killers," who terrorized California during the 1980s and '90s, leaving up to 30 victims in their wake.

Although Herzog was convicted of three murders and was given what was essentially a life sentence, the convictions were thrown out on technicalities and he was allowed to plead guilty to manslaughter, which allowed him to be released from prison after serving only 11 years. Many people were relieved when Herzog took his own life in 2012.

Thomas Kokoraleis is another known serial killer who was released from prison. Kokoraleis was a member of the notorious Chicago "Ripper Crew," who were responsible for murdering, raping, and torturing at least 18 women as part of Satanic rituals. Kokoraleis' brother Andrew was executed in 1999, but Thomas was released on parole by the Illinois Department of Corrections in March 2019. Other than those two cases, you have to look far and wide to find examples of known serial killers being released from prison and most of them are in developing countries.

Another major exception to the rule is American Marybeth Tinning. Like Megan Huntsman, Marybeth Tinning preyed on her children, killing eight of them over nearly 15 years. None of Tinning's children were safe—she killed her sons and daughters and showed no particular preference. Unlike Huntsman, Tinning had plenty of support as she went to trial, did time in prison, and after she was ultimately released. Yes, Marybeth Tinning, a woman who murdered eight of her children, was recently released from a women's prison in the state of New York.

As some still struggle to understand why Marybeth Tinning kept killing her children, over and over, others wonder how she got away with it for so long. Still many also wonder how a person who committed such heinous acts could ever be released from prison.

Duanesburg, New York

Marybeth Tinning was born Marybeth Roe in Duanesburg, New York on September 11, 1942. Duanesburg is today a small town in north-central New York, but when Marybeth was born, it was a lot more active. Many of the young men of the area, including Marybeth's father, went off to fight in Europe and the Pacific during World War II, while their sisters, mothers, and wives contributed by working in area factories.

When the war was over, Marybeth's father returned home and took a job in one of the area factories. Life was stable for her for the most part in the 1950s and early 1960s—she got everything she needed in terms of material possessions and Duanesburg was a safe and quiet town.

Marybeth wasn't a standout student in terms of academics, but she did stand out for her looks. By her late teens, Marybeth was 5'4 and petite with blonde hair and blue eyes. The usually quiet girl could've had her pick of young men in the area, but she chose Joe Tinning. Although Joe Tinning wasn't exactly the most charismatic, best looking, or most ambitious guy in town, he was pretty stable. He was a hard worker and wasn't known to drink much or womanize. He was exactly the type of guy a woman looking to settle down in the 1960s would want.

The two began dating and married in 1965. Joe worked in area factories while Marybeth worked as a nurse's aide in nearby Schenectady. Everything seemed to be going well, but underneath the surface, there were problems from the start. Marybeth was a bit of a jealous woman and also fairly paranoid. When Joe came home late from work or from hanging out with his friends, she would give him the third degree, or accuse him of cheating on her. By the early 1970s, Joe was thinking about leaving Marybeth.

But not before Marybeth decided to take things into her own hands. In 1974, in the middle of the marriage problems that the two were having and after they had already lost three of their children under suspicious circumstances, Marybeth gave Joe a near-deadly dose of barbiturates. The poisoning was discovered after Joe went to the emergency room and the police were called, but in a pattern that would repeat itself for the subsequent 30 years, Joe refused to hold his wife accountable. The incident illustrated the relationship that Mary and Joe had and the power dynamics that were at work. Mary was the one who wore the pants in the Tinning family.

Although Joe may have been a spineless individual who let his wife walk over him and kill their children, the police should have known better. The poisoning should have been a wakeup call for the authorities to investigate more, especially considering that three of the Tinning children had already died.

But law enforcement was very different in 1974 than it is today. If the victim didn't want to pursue matters, then the police and the

70

prosecutors usually wouldn't. Unfortunately for the Tinning children, this meant that the police wouldn't interfere in the Tinning household for over ten more years.

Living and Dying in the Tinning Home

Most people who work in the health care industry are nurturing types. They enter the field because they care about their fellow humans and want to help by alleviating suffering. Marybeth Tinning was a healthcare worker who, on the outside, appeared to be a very caring person. She was diligent at her job and was well-liked by her fellow workers and her patients. But underneath that surface was a very disturbed, very violent person.

Tinning had a deep urge to kill, but instead of preying on her patients as an "angel of death" would do, she preferred to enact her murderous desires on her family.

Barbara was the first child the Tinnings had. She was born in 1967, about two years after Joe and Marybeth were married. By all accounts, she was a happy child and the Tinnings seemed to be quite happy together. Marybeth was outwardly a good mother, doting on Barbara whenever they were in public.

In 1970, Joe Junior was born and it seemed as though the Tinning family was well on their way to being an all-American family. Marybeth told her family and friends that she planned to have more children, but the reality was that there were plenty of problems beneath the surface. Marybeth began giving Joe a hard time by the early 1970s while masking her darker side in public. By 1971, Marybeth Tinning was about to begin her domestic killing spree.

The Tinnings welcomed their third child, Jenifer, to the family in December 1971. Marybeth appeared happy to have her third child, but a mere eight days later she brought Jenifer into the local emergency room unresponsive. Jenifer was dead, and after a cursory examination, the doctors ruled that she had died from hemorrhagic meningitis and brain abscesses.

It was truly a tragedy, but life went on in the Tinning home. Joe and Marybeth had to go back to work to take care of their two surviving children. Friends, family, and neighbors of the Tinnings said that Jenifer's death bothered both of them but that they were dealing with the situation as best they could.

Just over a year later, on January 20, 1972, Joe Junior was brought to the emergency room unresponsive. He died that night of what was ruled cardiopulmonary arrest—he stopped breathing. The chances of lightning striking twice in the same home are extremely low, but just a few weeks after Joe Junior died, it struck the Tinnings a third time. Barbara, who was not quite five, was brought in unresponsive and later died. Her death was ruled to be the result of Reyes syndrome.

To an outsider, it would look like, in the early 1970s, the Tinning family were either very unlucky or something nefarious was taking place. The reality was that something nefarious was indeed taking place: Marybeth was killing her children, one at a time, but no one—including her husband—seemed to suspect her. Perhaps it was her quiet demeanor or possibly the fact that she worked in healthcare that kept the local doctors and police from digging just beneath the surface. After all, Marybeth Tinning and her husband were pillars of the Schenectady area, so nothing bad could be taking place.

Besides, truly bad things only happened down in New York City, the doctors and police of Schenectady probably thought.

Any doubts the local doctors and law enforcement had about Marybeth Tinning was gradually forgotten because the Tinnings didn't have any more children for Marybeth to kill. They remained childless for over a year until Marybeth became pregnant again in early 1973. Marybeth gave birth to her fourth child, Timothy, on Thanksgiving Day 1973.

She brought Timothy home, and to Marybeth's and Joe's friends and family, it seemed as though it would be a happy holiday season. It looked as though the couple had turned the corner from their early tragic losses and that the addition of Timothy to their family would at least partially make up for them.

But on December 10, just about two weeks after Timothy was born, Marybeth brought him to the hospital unresponsive. Marybeth was beginning to become a regular customer at the Schenectady County hospital, but once again, there seemed to be a legitimate, albeit tragic explanation for her child's death.

Timothy's body showed no outward signs of trauma and since he just quit breathing, as Marybeth claimed, he was ruled the victim of "crib death" or Sudden infant death syndrome (SIDS).

The tragic deaths of the Tinning children became the talk of many people around Schenectady, including the friends and family of Marybeth and Joe. Although many in the area began to question how so many tragic coincidences could happen in the same family, those closest to the couple continued to support them.

Then the news came that Marybeth was again pregnant. After Nathan was born on March 30, 1975, which happened to be Easter Sunday that year, friends and family of the Tinnings nervously awaited tragedy to strike. But after a few months, it seemed as though Nathan would make it until he too was struck by the Tinning curse.

On September 2, 1975, Marybeth came to the emergency room in Schenectady with an unresponsive Nathan. She told the doctors that Nathan just quit breathing and that she rushed him to the hospital as fast as she could. The doctors couldn't revive Nathan, and based on the fact that he had no outward trauma, combined with the story Marybeth gave them, they ruled that he too was the victim of SIDS.

The SIDS diagnosis should've raised multiple red flags. Although the

73

study and knowledge of SIDS was still relatively new in the 1970s, the doctors of Schenectady County were aware of SIDS since they ruled it the cause of Timothy's and Nathan's deaths. More importantly, since those doctors were aware of what SIDS was, they also would've known that it is not a genetic condition. The chances of multiple babies dying from it in the same family would be rare, and if it happened, it would either be the result of woeful neglect or premeditation.

Still, no serious questions were raised by local officials about the activities in the Tinning home.

Sure, She Can Adopt a Child

The years went on and the few people in the Schenectady area who were suspicious of Marybeth Tinning and her perishing children eventually forgot. Even the people who were supposed to defend the children of New York forgot or failed to do their due diligence in investigating Marybeth's background when she applied to adopt a child.

Yes, you heard that right, Marybeth and Joe Tinning applied to adopt a child in 1978. The adoption process was much the same in the late 1970s as it is today. Anyone wanting to go through the process was required to submit to a background check by the state, which included a complete examination of the adoptee's criminal and financial records. Since neither Marybeth nor Joe had criminal records and they were both gainfully employed, they easily passed the first round of the adoption process.

A social worker then interviewed the couple and visited their home to make sure it was suitable for a child. The Tinnings also passed this part of the process with flying colors. One would think that the fact that all five of the Tinnings' children died before the age of five would've been a red flag to the social workers investigating the adoption. But Marybeth assured them that they were all natural deaths and that she had the doctor's records to prove it.

The adoption process was directly related to the deaths of her children, Marybeth argued, stating that there was something wrong with her or Joe and that, although they both still wanted children, it would be safer to adopt.

The state of New York agreed and allowed the Tinnings to adopt an infant boy who they named Michael in 1978. But as the Tinnings were going through the adoption process, Marybeth became pregnant once more and gave birth to a girl, Mary Frances, on October 29, 1978. The arrival of Mary Frances meant that the Tinnings had two children in the home at the same time. It was certainly a different situation for them, but to those who knew them, they seemed to handle it well. Family and friends thought that Marybeth and Joe were finally on their way to having the family they always wanted.

In January, though, the horrible pattern repeated itself when Marybeth brought Mary Frances to the emergency room unresponsive. Then, in another twist to this very tragic case, the doctors were able to revive Mary Frances and send her home to her parents.

Unfortunately, coming home was a death sentence for Mary Frances. A month later, Marybeth brought Mary Francis into the hospital again, but the doctors were unable to revive her the second time. It appears Marybeth Tinning *made sure* that her child wouldn't survive the second time.

But Marybeth Tinning was far from done having children, or from murdering them. The Tinnings welcomed Jonathan to their family on November 19, 1979, and in March 1980, he was brought to the hospital in much the same condition as all of his previously doomed siblings. Medical professionals in Schenectady County took a second and third look at this case. It was now the 1980s and a new generation of healthcare workers who didn't know the Tinnings were in charge of things and computers made it easy for them to quickly look up records.

The Schenectady County healthcare professionals were concerned about all the deaths in the Tinning family but still thought that maybe it was genetically related. Others thought that maybe it had something to do with the family home. Still, no one suspected Marybeth yet. And for whatever reason, Joe never seemed to suspect a thing either. The concerned professionals in Schenectady County decided to send little Jonathan to Boston where he could be examined by specialists. The specialists could find nothing wrong so they sent him home, where he died on March 24, 1980.

Jonathan's death was the straw that broke the camel's back for many Schenectady County healthcare and law enforcement officials. The sheer number of deaths in the Tinning family was enough alone to cause suspicions, but the deaths also seemed to fit a pattern. Most of the children died in the fall, winter, and early spring months, and two were killed on holidays.

The dates of the deaths could suggest that depression played a role, but 1980 was still a few years before experts knew a lot about clinical depression, so all suspicions remained purely speculative. Those suspicions began to grow when Marybeth brought Michael to the family's pediatrician on March 2, 1981. Marybeth told the doctor that Michael went to sleep and she couldn't wake him up. The doctor didn't need to look at the child very long to see that he was dead.

Eight of Marybeth Tinning's children were now dead. Michael's death piqued the interest of even more officials because he was brought to the family's pediatrician instead of the emergency room, but even more so because he was adopted, proving that the Tinning curse couldn't be genetic. But Marybeth Tinning would claim one last victim before she was finally brought to justice.

The IQ level and culpability of Joe Tinning need to be seriously questioned at this point. Any normal husband of an average IQ would seriously begin questioning the role of his wife in the deaths of *all* his children, especially if he considered that his wife was the last person to be with the child before each death. Based on that alone, one would have to think that the husband in question was either really stupid or possibly involved in the crime. Or maybe just pathetic.

By all accounts, it seems that Joe was that pathetic. Maybe he *thought* something was going on, but he was too weak to do or say anything. Remember, this is the same guy who was poisoned by his wife yet he not only refused to have her prosecuted but took her back with open arms. Joe desired the stability of marriage over the lives of his children and therefore just kept going through the motions of the murderous charade that began in the early 1970s.

By 1985, Joe Tinning certainly had to think something was going on in his house. He definitely would've had to have tried hard to ignore the carnage that had been taking place underneath his roof. In 1985, the Tinnings welcome their last child into their home, Tami Lynne. At this point, people around Schenectady were wondering about the Tinnings and their seemingly endless procession of dead children.

On December 19, 1985, Tami Lynne became the final child to die at Marybeth's hands. Unlike all of the previous Tinning children, who were brought to the hospital, Tami Lynne was discovered dead in the Tinning home by a neighbor. There seemed to be no credible reason for the child's death, which led to the police to seriously consider foul play and Marybeth as a suspect.

"I Smothered Them with a Pillow"

The Schenectady County Sheriff's Department finally started taking a serious look at Marybeth Tinning after her ninth child died. The fact that nine of her children died under her care was bad enough, but what made things worse and more suspicious was that *all* of her children died under her watch.

The investigators began asking questions of the doctors and nurses who had treated Tinning and her children before making their way to friends and family of the Tinnings and then finally Marybeth herself. Marybeth knew what was coming when she went into the sheriff's department for questioning and it didn't take long for her to confess.

"I smothered them with a pillow," Tinning said about Tami Lynne, Nathan, and Timothy. She claimed to have not remembered much about the murders and never gave a real reason, but it was enough to charge her with murder and bring her to trial. Marybeth Tinning was convicted of one count of second-degree murder on July 17, 1987, and sentenced to 20 years to life in prison.

But there were still many unanswered questions about the case, particularly: did Marybeth Tinning kill all nine of her children? The people of north-central certainly wanted to know the answer and so did the authorities, so the bodies of the babies were exhumed.

Although the exhumations and subsequent examinations of the children never led to more charges, they did reveal another interesting aspect of the case. As discussed earlier, Joe Tinning's behavior during his wife's killing spree was important because he was either woefully ignorant or complicit in the crimes.

When his children were being exhumed, though, Joe Tinning didn't seem to care. "I wouldn't like them to do any more," said Joe to a reporter while the graves were being exhumed. "But I guess that's their prerogative." Certainly, a strange thing to say, but perhaps not so strange when you consider that, according to the forensic examiner who examined the nine children's bodies, Joe had "difficulty remembering all their names."

Marybeth was sent to the women's maximum-security prison in Bedford Hills, New York to serve her time, but was not forgotten by the people of Schenectady County. With that said, the people of north-central New York moved on with their lives without Tinning.

All except one of them. Yes, strangely enough—or perhaps not based on what we now know about him—Joe Tinning continued to support his wife. He drove down to visit her regularly and never even considered divorce. For her part, Marybeth avoided major problems with other inmates and staff in prison, although she wasn't very popular among her peers due to the nature of her crimes.

Finally, due to her time served as she awaited trial and changes in the "good time" status in the New York Department of Corrections, Marybeth Tinning was eligible for parole in 2007. Surely she wouldn't be released, would she?

Well, she was denied parole largely due to statements she made herself. Marybeth refused to take responsibility for what she did, stating that she didn't remember much of the murder. After she was denied parole, though, she was eligible to go before the board every two years, and in that time, several things changed.

Besides her husband, Marybeth Tinning started gaining some supporters who believed that she was a victim of the psychological disorder Munchausen syndrome by proxy. Her supporters argued that Marybeth Tinning was the victim of mental illness and a perfect example of how those afflicted with mental illness once used to fall through the cracks. They argued that, if she were younger, in the current system, she would've been caught and received treatment after her first child died.

It's hard to say if any of that would be true, but the arguments did gain the support of some influential people. Tinning's supporters petitioned the parole board and helped her craft better responses to the parole board's questions.

"After the deaths of my other children…I just lost it," she admitted to the parole board on January 26, 2011. "[I] became a damaged worthless piece of person, and when my daughter was young, in my state of mind at that time, I just believed she was going to die. So I just did it." She still only took responsibility for killing Tami Lynne, but it was certainly an improvement in the eyes of the parole board.

Andrew Cuomo was elected governor of New York in 2010 and immediately embarked on a program of progressive reforms throughout the state. One of the primary areas of reform that Cuomo focused on was prison reform, particularly making it easier for inmates to get parole. Cuomo's prison reform was certainly controversial and ended with several notorious gang members, cop killers, and drug kingpins getting released, but in liberal New York state, the voters were for the most part behind the efforts.

Among the wave of career criminals who were released was an old lady who most people in north-central New York had forgotten about and many younger people had never heard of—Marybeth Tinning.

Marybeth Tinning was released from prison on August 21, 2018. She was reunited with her husband and moved back to the Schenectady area, where she'll be under state supervision for the rest of her life. One of the many provisions of her release prohibits her from being around children.

Hopefully, she follows that provision.

CHAPTER 8

DEBRA JENNER-TYLER, THE HEARTLAND CHILD KILLER

If you've ever been to Huron, South Dakota, then you know that not much happens in the small town. Huron has a Walmart, a few churches, a public school, and not much else. It is very much like many other towns in eastern South Dakota, known as "East River" by South Dakotans. Huron is much like small towns in Iowa, Minnesota, Missouri, or any number of towns in the American Midwest. The people are friendly, if not a little nosy, crime is low, and so too is the cost of living. Most of the people of Huron like living there, as it is a much slower pace of life than nearby Sioux Falls, never mind Minneapolis or Omaha, both of which are a few hours' drive away.

You will generally meet two types of people in Huron. The first are those who moved there to get away from the big city. These people took pay cuts to live in a smaller town, are self-employed, or retired to Huron. Huron to these people is a slice of heaven that is uncorrupted by urban sprawl and decay.

The second and largest group is people who are from Huron or one of the nearby towns. Huron is the heart of South Dakota's farm country and much of the major money in the town is connected to farming. Although large, corporate farms have become more common in South Dakota in recent decades, many of the farms in the Huron area have been handed down from generation to generation. Farming is truly in the blood of the people of the area and much of the town's economy focuses on serving the farmers. People from these two groups do share many things. Most tend to be politically conservative, more religious than average, and truly enjoy living in the area.

Outside of some minor incidents, crime is not a big issue in Huron, South Dakota, so when the town received the news that a local woman had killed her child on April 5, 1987, the town and the state of South Dakota were gripped with fear and revulsion.

How could one of Huron's own do such a thing? Unfortunately, the answer to that question has never been obvious, although an examination of the story may help.

A Hometown Girl

Debra Jenner was a South Dakota girl, born and bred, so when she met and later married hometown boy Lynn Tyler, it seemed like they were the perfect match. They both attended the same church and had the same long-term goals—start a family and live happily ever after!

Debra gave birth to a son in 1983 and a daughter, Abby Lynn, in 1984. Everything seemed to be perfect in the Tyler home: Lynn had a good job, they were well-respected in the community, and the children were healthy.

But as with so many of these cases, there were problems underneath the surface.

Debra had mental health issues that weren't being addressed. Part of the problem was that she was good at masking them, but at the same time, mental health issues weren't readily addressed or talked about in rural South Dakota in the 1980s.

Debra was often withdrawn and sullen, but it was said to be the just part of the long winters of South Dakota or that she was going through a "phase." She continued to linger in a malaise until the fateful night of April 4, 1987.

The Murder

In April 1987, Abby Lynn Jenner was a 3-year-old girl with her whole life in front of her. She was the apple of her father's eye and was loved by her older brother. Debra also seemed to genuinely love Abby Lynn, which is what makes what happened on April 4 so perplexing.

April 4, 1987, was a cold Saturday night in Huron, South Dakota. The last vestiges of winter were still lingering and the days were only just starting to get a little longer. The Tyler's spent the night at home and Debra put both of the children to bed before 10:00 p.m. and then went to bed with Lynn.

Then, some time in the middle of the night, she woke up and entered Abby Lynn's room.

As Abby Lynn was sleeping, Debra attacked without saying a word. She attacked her poor, helpless child with a kitchen knife and also a toy airplane, of all things. Yes, Debra Jenner-Tyler used a toy airplane to stab her daughter to death.

Then, after murdering her daughter in a frenzy, Debra cleaned up and went back to bed.

Lynn got up early the next morning to get his family ready for church and was horrified to find a massacre in his daughter's room. Blood was splashed across every wall and laying in her bloody bed was the disfigured Abby Lynn.

The Beadle County Sheriff's Department and the Huron Police were immediately called to the scene. It was the most brutal crime scene any of the responding officers, or the detectives who investigated the case later had seen. Sure, Huron had some crime and even an occasional murder, but nothing like this.

The people of Huron immediately had theories of their own.

Some thought it was the work of a cult, while others believed it was done by an itinerant serial killer.

The investigators working the case, though, had other ideas.

Debra initially told the responding officers that an intruder had committed the murder, but when pressed for further details, such as a description of the killer or at what time the murder took place, she could offer nothing. She then said the night was a blur and that she couldn't tell them anything else.

Since Debra hadn't been drinking or taking any drugs that night, there was no real reason for her memory to be blurry, unless she had something to hide.

Debra went to the police station two days later for a longer, more formal interview and also to take a polygraph test. She failed miserably.

The Beadle County authorities knew right then who Abby Lynn's killer was.

Life in Prison?

Debra was convicted of second-degree murder in 1988 and sentenced to life in prison, which in South Dakota usually means exactly that. She was shipped off to the women's prison in Pierre where most people believed, and hoped, she would be forgotten. Her husband divorced her and she lost contact with her son.

For decades, Debra sat in prison, proclaiming her innocence to anyone who would listen, filing failed appeal after failed appeal. Then, in 2002, she got word that Governor Bill Janklow may hand out a bunch of pardons and commutations before his term was up in January 2003.

It was controversial, but Governor Janklow was already at that point quite a controversial figure. He had already served two terms as South Dakota's governor in the 1980s and had just completed his second term before Abby Lynn was murdered. He then ran for and won the governorship again in 1995 and served until he reached his term limit in 2002.

Before the second term of his second stint as governor, Janklow had been accused of rape by a girl on an Indian reservation in 1974. Janklow was never charged with any crime in the case and he went on to a successful and long career in South Dakota politics. As he worked his way up the political ladder, he earned him a reputation as a guy who did things in a way of his own.

And, as he left office in late 2002, he did some more things in a way of his own.

Janklow handed out several controversial pardons and commutations of criminal convictions, including his son-in-law for drunk driving and marijuana possession convictions. Perhaps the most controversial commutation was the one that reduced Debra Jenner-Tyler's sentence from life to 100 years. Although that may not seem like much of a commutation, it allowed her to be immediately eligible for parole.

The innocence that Jenner-Tyler claimed throughout the 1980s and '90s suddenly vanished—Debra became a contrite woman who wanted a second chance. "Am I sorry? Yes, every day," Jenner-Tyler told the parole board in 2003. "I wish it could have been me."

A lot of people in South Dakota also wished it would have been Debra, who now in her sixties stands little chance of being released. The very conservative nature of the state is one strike against her, but maybe even more so is the legacy left behind by Bill Janklow. Just months after her sentence was commuted, Bill Janklow killed a motorcycle rider in a car accident. Janklow was convicted of vehicular manslaughter and served time in jail. He died in 2012 and is often remembered in the state for the man he killed in 2003, the people he released from prison in 2002, and the questions about his activities on the Rosebud Indian Reservation in the 1970s.

None of that bodes well for Debra Jenner-Tyler's parole chances in the future.

CHAPTER 9

THE MILITARY MOM MURDERESS, JULIE SCHENECKER

One of the most commonly said phrases after any family massacre is, "I should've seen it coming." These words are uttered by family and friends of the killer who claim to have witnessed conversations, behavior, and incidents that should have tipped them off to the subsequent violence. The reality is that these people usually are telling the truth; family massacres don't just happen one day. They are usually the end of a long process that has been building for days, weeks, months, or even years. And usually someone involved tries to get help.

Often a concerned family member will attempt to tell others about the impending doom and sometimes the family member is an abused child. Unfortunately, the cries for help are often ignored, and even when they are investigated, they are not taken very seriously.

The family member being accused of abuse can often talk their way out of the situation. It helps when the family member being accused is a woman and one who doesn't appear to be the stereotypical child abuser. If the woman being accused happens to be well-groomed, middle-class, articulate, and comes from a military background, then investigators are going to be prone to believe the accused. The situation can often lead to tragic results, as it did in Tampa, Florida on January 27, 2011.

In the months before that date, 16-year-old Calyx Schenecker filed an official abuse complaint against her mother, 49-year-old Julie

Schenecker. Although Calyx showed no visible, physical signs of abuse, social workers were sent to the Schenecker home to investigate. The home was clean and orderly and located in a nice, upper-middle-class neighborhood of Tampa. The investigators found Julie intelligent, warm, and engaging, not at all what they were used to with similar cases that sent them to housing projects and trailer parks. She was, after all, a military veteran, and her husband was an active high-ranking officer in the Army. The case against Julie Schenecker was quickly dropped.

The Hillsborough County social workers quickly forgot about Julie Schenecker until they heard the first news reports on January 28, 2011. Those who remembered the case were shocked and mortified to learn that the seemingly normal mother they had met months earlier stood accused of brutally murdering her two children. The county social workers should've seen it coming.

Two Overachievers

If you had known Julie Schenecker in the 1970s or '80s, there is no way you would've thought that one day she would stand accused of killing her children. She was a good daughter, an excellent student, and an all-around go-getter.

Julie Schenecker was born Julie Powers on January 13, 1961, to a middle-class family in the small town of Muscatine, Iowa. Many of Julie's friends and those with whom she went to school in the southeastern Iowa town were born into farm life and would remain in the area for their entire lives. Julie liked the area and her family, but she always knew she was destined for something greater. She did well in school and earned a scholarship to attend the University of Northern Iowa in Cedar Falls.

Julie adapted well to college life, maintaining top grades while she played volleyball and other sports. She also developed an extensive social network but had little time for the party lifestyle. Julie had big plans in life and keg parties weren't going to get her where she wanted to be.

When graduation came, Julie decided to take a slightly different path than most of her peers. She had done exceptionally well with foreign languages in college, which was noted by a recruiter for the United States Army. The recruiter sold Julie on the benefits of Army life, including numerous career opportunities when her hitch was done.

Upon graduation, Julie enlisted and was sent to West Germany to be a Russian linguist. Her skills and education were in high demand in the late 1980s, during the Cold War, which often put her in the same room with high-ranking officers. One of those officers was Parker Schenecker.

Although Parker Schenecker also came from a middle-class background, his family was career military so they moved around quite a bit during his youth. The Scheneckers never stayed in one place very long, which can be difficult for the children of some military families, but young Parker seemed to thrive on the perennial adventure. Parker followed his father's career path and after graduating from college he became an officer. He was truly happy with his life, but he wanted someone with whom to share it.

As Parker was moving his way up the ranks of the Army, eventually earning the rank of colonel, he met Julie at a base in Munich in the late 1980s. The two immediately hit it off and seemed to be a good match: both were intelligent, ambitious people who were seemingly going to do great things with their lives. They were also close to the same age and shared a desire to start a family. But the Scheneckers wedded bliss didn't last long.

Growing Problems

After marrying, the Scheneckers became a typical military family. Parker was steadily moving forward with his career and had big plans to make

88

general one day, while Julie planned to be the dutiful military wife and mother. But almost immediately there were signs that the Scheneckers' picture-perfect military life had some major problems.

Perhaps the constant moving around was too much for Julie. After all, she was a Midwestern girl who was accustomed to stability. Many people find military life stressful, and by the early 1990s, Julie appeared ready to crack.

Julie was diagnosed with depression and given medication, which seemed to work. The couple then had daughter Calyx in 1994 and son Beau in 1997. The combination of the medication and raising the couple's two children seemed to bring Julie out of her depression, but when the Schenecker kids became teens, everything started all over again.

By the early 2000s, the Scheneckers had moved to a nice neighborhood in Tampa, Florida, but Parker was often gone, sometimes for long periods, due to his work. Julie's depression came back in 2001 so severely that she was hospitalized briefly that year. But she returned home ready to be the wife and mother that she once was, although, by the late 2000s, her husband was frequently in the Middle East. The situation meant that Julie had to often shoulder the majority of the parental duties, which was for her becoming untenable due to the physical, emotional, and social changes that come with puberty and being a teen. Julie and Calyx especially had numerous battles.

As is often typical in a parent-teen relationship, Julie took issue with Calyx's friends, music, and clothes, while Calyx never backed down and was always willing to confront her mother. She had inherited a bit of stubbornness from both of her parents. The arguments between Julie and Calyx would get pretty heated, with threats sometimes bandied about, but in one confrontation in late 2010, Julie stepped over the line and hit her daughter. Calyx was probably angrier and feeling hurt that her mother had hit her rather than being physically injured, but she still decided to call the police. The police came to the Schenecker residence and filed a report, but after speaking with Julie, they decided to leave and not push the matter any further. Julie Schenecker, after all, was a military mom, a paragon of American values! She was also a very disturbed woman.

Saving Her Children

Career military people tend to be very regimented and disciplined, which can be good when it comes to long-term planning, but not when unexpected problems arise. With that said, the problems between Julie and Calyx were not necessarily unexpected and were part of a long-festering process that began before the Scheneckers had children.

But this was not part of Parker's long-term plans and goals, so he refused to acknowledge what was about to unfold in front of him. As the conflict between Julie and Calyx reached a volatile crescendo, Parker did what many familiar with the case thought was inexplicable—he left the country. In fairness to Parker, he was a high-ranking officer in the Army, so when duty called, he had to go, no questions asked. So, when Parker received orders to go to the Middle East in the middle of January 2011, he went.

The career military man didn't seem to have created a contingency plan for his family when he left, which is a bit strange when one considers his background. Maybe he just wanted to get away from the situation and hoped that it would all work itself out while he was gone. The situation certainly did work itself out but not in the way he would've wanted.

While Parker was away, Julie outwardly went about her daily routine. She brought her kids to and from school and did her other errands, with one extra one on the week of January 27—she bought a .38 caliber pistol. Based on her record of mental illness, Julie probably shouldn't have been able to get a gun, but she did, allowing her to put her diabolical plan into action.

January 27 started like any other day in the Schenecker home. It was a school day, so Beau and Calyx went to school, while Julie spent the day doing errands. Julie was planning to "save" her children that day.

When Beau returned home from school he probably didn't notice anything out of the ordinary about his mom. Julie carefully concealed what she was about to do, as she didn't want her children to struggle or for things to get "messy."

Beau got ready for soccer practice and then got in the car as he did every other day. Julie made sure that her son was safely buckled in and then, after driving for a few miles, she methodically pulled the pistol out and shot her son twice, once in the face and once in the head. Julie then drove home to finish her mission.

The tension between Julie and Calyx had been extremely high since Calyx had called the police and it only got worse after Parker went to the Middle East. When the two talked, it usually ended in an argument, so by January 27 they were rarely speaking.

But Julie was done talking to Calyx at all that evening. She no longer had to hear what her daughter thought about anything and there would never again be a conflict between them. Just as she had done with Beau, Julie methodically stalked Calyx, waiting for the right time to kill her daughter.

Calyx was on the family's computer that evening, checking her social media and doing some schoolwork. As she was updating her latest post, Julie snuck up behind her and shot once, sending a bullet through the back of the girl's mouth. Julie then finished her off with a shot to the neck. Julie dragged Calyx's body to one of the bedrooms, where it appears that she intended to join her. She then overdosed on a combination of Lithium and Coumadin and wrote a suicide note.

"It was my time to go—heaven is waiting for me I have done my job on this earth. The best job I ever had was having/bringing up my babies.

This is why I had to bring them on with me. It's too possible they've inherited the DNA and live their lives depressed or bi-polar! I believe I've saved them from the pain," the note read.

Before Julie could fade away into death, a concerned family member called the police who arrived and were able to save her.

Resolution?

After spending a day in the hospital, Julie Schenecker was arrested and charged with two counts of first-degree murder for the brutal deaths of her two children. Schenecker was also charged with the lesser counts of second-degree murder and manslaughter and was held in the Hillsborough County jail with no bond. To make matters worse for Julie, the District Attorney's office announced that, due to the brutal nature of the crimes, they would seek the death penalty. In Florida, the death penalty is routinely given as a sentence and it is also carried out quite often.

Once the extent of Julie's mental illness was revealed, though, the DA decided to drop the death penalty but move forward with both murder charges. If convicted, Julie Schenecker would likely spend the rest of her life in a tough Florida prison.

Although Schenecker was glad to hear that she wouldn't be executed if convicted of her children's murders, she was further devastated when Parker filed for divorce in May 2011. Parker was justifiably angry with Julie and hurt to the extent that, after the potential trial, he never wanted to see her again.

Most people who followed Schenecker's case believed it was a slam dunk. After all, she had admitted to committing both murders. But Julie's attorneys were vigorous advocates on her behalf and decided to pursue an insanity defense. Over the last several decades, insanity defenses have rarely been tried in American courts and have been successful even less often. Still, Schenecker's defense attorneys knew that, based on their client's history of mental illness, they had an outside chance of a "not guilty by reason of insanity" verdict. It was wishful thinking.

When the jury read the verdict on May 15, 2014, it was guilty on all counts. Schenecker was later given two life sentences to be served concurrently, which means that she will more than likely die in prison. Before she was led away to prison after her sentencing, Julie took responsibility for her crimes, somewhat.

"I apologize. I apologize to everybody in this courtroom...the lives I have destroyed," Schenecker said as she cried. "I take responsibility. I was there. I know...I know I shot my son and daughter. I don't know why."

CHAPTER 10

ANDREA YATES, THE MENTALLY ILL TICKING TIME BOMB

As mentioned in the previous case, the insanity defense is rarely tried in American courts and is even less rarely successful when it is attempted. Each state of the Union has different laws and standards for when and how an insanity defense can be used, but it is attempted less than 1% of the time overall.

Although there has been a trend since the 1960s to treat mental illness with understanding and empathy, the American courts have somewhat gone the other way, viewing those who make mental illness claims with skepticism. Beginning in the 1990s, some states even banned the use of the insanity defense, which has been upheld by the United States Supreme Court.

Despite the much higher burden of proof and the general trend against the "insanity defense," it is still attempted from time to time and is on occasion successful. Generally speaking, those who are acquitted of murder charges by reason of insanity have a lot of evidence to support their claims. They have usually been committed to a mental health facility at least once and are often on medication.

But psychologists and psychiatrists who work in the criminal justice system will point out that even people afflicted with the worst cases of mental illness rarely commit acts of violence. Those who do are usually long-term sufferers of mental illness and are also subjected to devastating personal or professional events during their psychotic breakdowns.

Texas mother Andrea Yates was once such a person.

Andrea Yates' life was seemingly on the path to greatness in the early 1990s: she had a great career as a nurse, had just married an ambitious young man, and was about to start a large family. Within fewer than five years, though, everything quickly began collapsing for Andrea. She descended into a seemingly endless abyss of mental illness that nothing could cure. Finally, on June 20, 2001, Andrea transferred her misery to the most helpless members of her family—her five young children.

The massacre of the Yates children shocked America, but it also brought debates about mental illness to the forefront. As people debated the general topic of mental illness on talk shows and the Internet, Andrea Yates' lawyers decided to be become part of the less than 1% of all cases by filing an insanity defense. The results of the case have left people shaking their heads and wondering if justice was served.

A Complicated Girl

Andrea Yates was born on July 2, 1964, in the small town of Hallsville, Texas to Andrew and Jutta Kennedy. Not much happened—or still does happen—in Hallsville, but that was just the way Andrea's parents liked it. Hallsville was the type of community where everyone knew each other and where nearly everyone in town belonged to one of its many churches.

The Kennedys were strong Christians and tried to live their lives that way, not only with the type of values they taught their children and the things they did day-to-day but also in the *type* of family they raised.

They were true believers in the biblical proverb that man is to be fruitful and multiply.

Andrea was the youngest of five children, which meant that she always had older siblings to watch out for and care for her. She was well-cared for by her family, and at an early age, she showed signs of precociousness. Andrea always asked questions and did well in elementary and high school. She also got along well with other students and teachers.

Andrea was named the valedictorian of her 1982 graduating class, which was a moment of pride for everyone in the Kennedy family. But being the valedictorian was not just a senior year thing; she did well throughout her high school years grade-wise and was a member of the National Honor Society.

By most accounts, Andrea was quite well-rounded in her high school days. Besides excelling in academics, Andrea was fairly athletic and was the captain of her high school's girl's swim team. But beneath the exterior, the stable, successful, and ambitious young woman that she portrayed, Andrea had some serious problems.

She began suffering from bulimia in her teen years, which may have been brought on by a combination of wanting to fit in and having to stay in shape for sports. Bulimia is certainly a mental health condition that is taken very seriously today, but in the early 1980s, especially in rural east Texas, it wasn't something that was even considered. Many people would have thought it was a normal way for a young woman to keep her figure.

According to one of Andrea's high school friends, she was also suicidal, which would go along with the bulimia. Still, despite her early mental health issues, Andrea Kennedy was accepted into the University of Texas's nursing school. Just as she had done in high school, Andrea studied hard, avoided the parties, and graduated with top honors in 1986.

After graduating, Andrea moved to Houston to begin her career.

Rusty Yates

Russell "Rusty" Yates was born in 1965 in upstate New York. The Yates family moved to Tennessee not long after Rusty was born, which is where he spent most of his youth. In many ways, Rusty's childhood reflected Andrea's. He did well in school, was well-liked, and most importantly, was a Christian. But Rusty wasn't necessarily a "holy roller" or "Bible banger," at least, not until he went to college.

For most young people in the early 1980s, just as it is today, college is the first taste of freedom. When not in class, many college kids like to experiment with drugs, sex, and alcohol and generally rebel against how they were raised. But not Rusty Yates.

When Rusty Yates was accepted into Auburn University in Auburn, Alabama, he didn't go down there with parties, girls, or even football on his mind. Rusty was a goal-orientated young man who focused on his studies. And as an engineering student, his course of study was not easy. Rusty had to take plenty of math and physics courses, but he excelled in all of them.

Despite being a bookworm throughout college, Rusty did find time for extra-curricular activities. Rusty's idea of a good time on the weekend was reading scriptures with some friends and going to church. Like Andrea in Texas, Rusty's spiritual and religious beliefs were instilled in him as a child, but while he was at Auburn, he met a young, charismatic street preacher named Michael Peter Woroniekci. As a former college football linebacker, Woroniekci didn't look like the typical street preacher and he didn't sound like one either. Woroniekci preached a fundamentalist, fire and brimstone style of Christianity that was heavily influenced by the Old Testament.

Rusty Yates hung on every word of Woroniekci and carried his teachings with him when he moved to Texas in the late 1980s. Rusty's hard work and prayers paid off; he received a position as a NASA engineer and moved to Texas to start the next chapter of his life. But as a good Christian man, there was something missing—a wife.

Andrea Kennedy met Rusty Yates in the Houston apartment complex where they were both lived in the early 1990s. To everyone who knew them, they seemed a perfect match: both were young professionals, neither used alcohol or drugs and most importantly, both were fundamentalist Christians. The couple married in 1993 and immediately set out to fulfill their Christian duty by having a large family.

Building a Family

Soon after getting married, Andrea and Rusty settled into a quiet, suburban lifestyle. They bought a home in the city of Friendswood, Texas, which is located halfway between Houston and Galveston. Rusty brought in good money with his NASA position and Andrea was on the verge of giving up her nursing career for what she wanted to do—or at least what she thought she wanted to do—motherhood.

When Andrea announced that she was pregnant in the middle of 1993, everything looked great for the Yates family: Rusty was making good money, the couple seemed happy, and they were about to have their first of many children. Rusty worked long hours, often leaving Andrea alone, but it was all done out of sacrifice for their first child, Noah, who was born on February 26, 1994.

In late 1994, Rusty was offered another job in Florida that paid more, but it meant that they would be far away from the support of Andrea's family. Still, the offer was too good for Rusty to refuse, so he and Andrea moved to Seminole, Florida. They lived in a trailer in the upper-middle-class community, which in some ways symbolized the life that Andrea was beginning to live at the time—although not necessarily isolated, Andrea was apart from everyone else.

For his part, Rusty believed that all Andrea needed for company were her children, and since she was about to have the couple's second child in early 1995, he felt she had no reason to feel alone. John was born on December 15, 1995, and for a while, it seemed as though Andrea was happy. The couple waited a while to have their third child, and in that period, there are no signs that Andrea was suffering from any mental illness. It could simply be a case of Andrea hiding her problems, but based on the fact that she was not afraid to seek medical help in later years for her mental health issues, one can assume that she was alright in the mid-1990s.

Andrea had Paul on September 13, 1997, and within a few months, the situation changed again for the mother. It appears that she became used to the relative isolation of Florida, made some friends, and took to motherhood, but then Rusty was offered another position back in Houston, so he moved the family, no questions asked, back to where they started.

The move back to Texas was not good for Andrea. She gave birth to the couple's fourth child, Luke, on February 15, 1999, and not long after, things began to quickly unravel in the Yates house.

A Decaying Mental State

Despite being closer to her extended family and back in her home state, Andrea Yates' mental state quickly deteriorated in the weeks after Luke was born. Rusty worked long hours, so he was either too busy to notice the situation, or simply didn't want to admit what was taking place. It should have been pretty obvious, though, as Andrea became more withdrawn and didn't seem to care much about anything, even her children.

Finally, on June 17, 1999, Andrea attempted suicide with pills. Although some of Andrea's family members thought that it was possibly a "cry for help," many were convinced that it was a legitimate suicide attempt. Either way, Rusty finally decided that Andrea needed some help, so he made her see a psychiatrist. Andrea was prescribed antidepressants, which seemed to have no effect, as she later tried to kill herself with a knife.

Rusty and the other members of the Yates and Kennedy families didn't seem to know what to do, so they sent Andrea to a psychiatrist named

Dr. Eileen Starbranch. Dr. Starbranch diagnosed Andrea with postpartum psychosis and prescribed her Haldol.

The general public knew little about postpartum psychosis in 1999, but the medical community had been studying its effects and treatment for some time. Andrea seemed to react well to the Haldol along with therapy sessions. She seemed to be happier by late 1999/early 2000, but Starbranch was adamant with her that she shouldn't have any more children. "I could pretty much predict that Ms. Yates would have another episode of psychosis," Starbranch later recalled.

Despite Starbranch's warnings, Rusty and Andrea decided to move ahead with their plans to grow their family. On November 30, 2000, they welcomed their first and only daughter, Mary Deborah into the family. Almost as soon as Mary was born, Andrea slipped back into her depression and near-catatonic state. She had difficulties caring for her children, which was aggravated by other triggering factors that took place in her life.

The death of Andrea's father in March 2001 came as a particular shock to the already mentally fragile mother of five. Andrea was particularly close to her father, always looking to him as a source of support. She would regularly talk with her father on the phone and visit him in person as much as possible.

When Andrew Kennedy passed away, a part of Andrea went with him. Andrea quit taking Haldol after her father died and quickly descended into an abyss of mental illness from which she couldn't escape. And she was going to take several others down with her.

The Massacre in Clear Lake City

Although Rusty may not have understood what his wife was going through, he did make some efforts to alleviate her pain. He moved the family into a nice, comfortable home in the suburb of Clear Lake City, in the hope that it would help the overall situation. The home was in a nice neighborhood and close to parks and shopping, but none of that seemed to interest Andrea. She preferred to just sit in her room.

Things got so bad by early June 2001 that Andrea's doctor told Rusty that she needed to be monitored around the clock. So Rusty got together with people from both sides of the family to work out a "watch" schedule. When Rusty was at work, his mother or someone else would be there until he returned.

But Rusty was a stubborn guy and believed he could figure things out as well as any doctor. He began leaving Andrea alone at home for longer periods each day, which he believed would eventually ween or train her to overcome her postpartum psychosis.

June 20, 2001, was one of those days. There was only to be one hour of lag time between when Rusty left for work and when his mom arrived to watch over Andrea and the children. But one hour was more than enough time for Andrea to carry out the mass prolicide.

As soon as Rusty left for work, Andrea filled one of the houses' bathtubs and began calling the children to the bathroom one at a time. First was John, who didn't think anything was out of the ordinary when his mother put his head under the water one last time.

Next came Paul and then Luke, both of whom she was able to dispatch fairly quickly. She then laid their bodies in their beds. Baby Mary came next. Just after drowning Mary, Andrea's oldest son, and the last survivor, Noah, asked, "What's wrong with Mary?" when he saw his infant sister floating in the tub.

He tried to make a run for it but Andrea chased him down, brought him back to the bathroom, and drowned Noah as she had done with all of his siblings. Andrea then took Mary's corpse and put it in John's arms. She left Noah floating in the tub.

It remains a mystery why Noah was left in the tub while his siblings were all ceremonially placed in their beds. Perhaps Andrea was angry at him for trying to resist her mass murder. Or maybe there was no real reason for it other than that his mother was unhinged. What took place next seems to confirm the unhinged theory.

Andrea took no steps to hide what she had done. There isn't any way that a person can conceal a mass murder, but she could've attempted to make it look like the work of an intruder, as so many other killers have done.

Instead, Andrea calmly called the police and told them to come to the address. She then called Rusty at work and only said, "It's time," before ending the call. Andrea Yates was arrested at the scene on suspicion of first-degree murder and brought to the Harris County jail for booking.

The First Trial

As Yates was being brought downtown to the police station, the responding officers secured the scene and the detectives who arrived later were horrified by what they saw. Hardened detectives who had seen plenty of crime and violence on the mean streets of Harris County, Texas had difficulties composing themselves. The Yates' neighbors in the normally quiet neighborhood emerged from their homes curious about the situation and were equally shocked when they learned about the circumstances.

Meanwhile, at the police station, Andrea didn't try to hide what she had done and offered a complete, albeit bizarre confession. "My children weren't righteous. They stumbled because I was evil. The way I was raising them they could never be saved," Andrea said. "They were doomed to perish in the fires of hell."

The detectives and the prosecutors who heard the confession were perplexed, but it was surely enough to charge and probably convict of five counts of capital murder. And, in Texas, capital murder means that, if convicted, the accused will probably face capital punishment.

Yates was put in a protective wing of the Harris County jail and not given bond. She would either beat the case against her and walk out the door of the courthouse or be sent to prison for the rest of her life or to die of lethal injection. There was a minuscule chance, though, that Andrea was not guilty by reason of insanity.

The prosecution's strategy was to rely totally on the evidence, which unequivocally showed that Andrea murdered her five children. The prosecution was under no obligation to prove a motive, but they did imply that Andrea murdered her children as part of some type of twisted spousal revenge.

The prosecution never brought up Andrea's mental state.

The defense had little to work with and was forced to try an insanity defense. Andrea's lawyers showed the documentation of her long battle with mental illness and called numerous friends and family, as well as her doctors, to the stand to testify on her behalf. The defense lawyers also cast blame on Woroniekci as a cult leader who takes advantage of people's mental conditions.

The jury seemed swayed by some of the defense's arguments and Andrea looked somewhat sympathetic as she sat next to her lawyers, sobbing. Pathetic may be a better word than sympathetic, but she did seem to be eliciting a certain amount of sympathy, or pity, from the jury.

In March 2002, the trial ended and the jury returned their verdict— guilty on all counts. Although Yates was convicted of all the murders, it was somewhat of a split verdict. The jury agreed that Yates' mental state played a role in the murder and was therefore a mitigating factor in her sentence of life in prison instead of the death penalty. But what kind of life could a woman who murdered all five of her children expect to have behind bars?

The Second Trial

Yates entered the Texas prison system with a large target on her back. Although women's prisons are far less violent than men's prisons in the United States, they are full of mothers separated from their children. Most of those women are serving time on charges other than child abuse, so when a woman who killed all five of her children is introduced into the population, it is sure to rankle some of the inmates.

Andrea kept her head down and avoided trouble. She was given various medications that seemed to improve her mental state, enough that she was able to work with her attorneys on her appeal. But what grounds did Yates have to appeal? After all, Yates' lawyers put up a spirited insanity defense, but it was rejected by a legitimate jury. Yates' lawyers were thorough enough, though, to find a technicality.

One of the prosecution's key witnesses in the trial was high profile forensic psychiatrist Dr. Park Dietz. By 2002, Dietz had built an impressive professional reputation from private practice early in his career and then as a professional expert witness in several high profile criminal cases. He testified for the prosecution in the trial of John Hinckley Junior's attempted murder of President Ronald Reagan and in the Jeffrey Dahmer trial. In both cases, he refuted the defense's arguments that their clients were insane. He was one for one in those trials.

In the Yates trial, Dietz argued that Andrea was not insane because she got the idea to drown her children from an episode of the hit television show *Law and Order*. The only problem was that no such episode had aired before Andrea killed her children. The Texas Court of Appeals thought that the false testimony given by Dietz was a miscarriage of justice, so on January 6, 2005, it threw out all verdicts from Andrea's first trial, which meant that the entire process would take place again.

In many similar cases, the prosecution often offers a plea deal to the defendant of much less time in prison, but in Andrea's case, no such deal was in the works. Instead, her attorneys decided to pursue a historically based defense strategy.

Daniel M'Naghten murdered another man in England in 1843. M'Naghten was found not guilty by reason of insanity by the jury in one of the first recorded such cases in the English-speaking world. The verdict would later influence courts in other English-speaking countries, including the United States, to accept "not guilty by reason of insanity," or other similarly worded verdicts, as a legitimate court verdict. Although many U.S. states had begun moving away from what is known as the "M'Naghten Rule" after World War II, Texas was not one of those states.

When Andrea Yates was brought back to Harris County in January 2006, the first incredible turn in what would be more than a few interesting turns in her case took place. To the surprise of everyone in the courtroom, and nearly everyone in America for that matter, the judge Turnered Andrea bail!

There were of course strict provisions for her bail: she had to wear a monitoring device, had to check in regularly with an officer of the court, and was prohibited from being around children. Still, the fact that she was given bail on five murder charges signaled which way the judge was leaning, which didn't look good for the prosecution.

Another interesting turn in the case involved Rusty Yates. Rusty was, of course, devastated at losing all five of his children, and he filed for divorce from Andrea in 2004, which was made official in 2005. In the true Christian spirit of forgiveness, he continued to support her in her quest for a new trial. "What happened to my family will always be with me and associated with me," Rusty said in a 2004 interview. "But I would like people to know we had a great family. I'd like people to know that something good can come from all this, and I want to be a part of it." Although Rusty never clearly articulated what the "good" was that would come from the tragedy, he was vocal in his opinion that Andrea should be in a mental health facility, not a prison.

Andrea's trial finally got underway in the summer of 2006 and in a courtroom that was much more subdued than the first trial, the jury returned a verdict of not guilty by reason of insanity on July 26, 2006. The public was truly stunned by this latest turn in the Andrea Yates mass murder case.

Andrea was sent to the North Texas State Hospital in Vernon, Texas, where she remains to this day. But most people were wondering at the time—and still are—what the sentence exactly means. Does it mean that Andrea Yates, one of America's most notorious mass murderers, will be allowed back on the streets one day?

Attorney and former Court TV anchor, Jean Casarez, explained the implication for her audience in 2006 after the verdict was announced. "At some point, because the court will have continuing jurisdiction over her case, she could go before a judge with doctors, with an attorney, to say that she is no longer a harm to herself or others, and at that point, she could be released," said Casarez. "Take John Hinckley...It took 21 years, but now he has home visits three and four nights at a time with his family."

If Andrea Yates is ever released, it would truly be the biggest turn yet in an incredibly tragic and bizarre case.

CHAPTER 11
PLAYING "CHICKEN" WITH HER CHILDREN, LEXUS STAGG

So far in this book, all of the cases profiled have featured mothers who killed their children in a pre-meditated manner, sometimes due to mental illness but always in a way that demonstrated great malice.

Although the next case is no less tragic, it is one where the victim died as a result of irresponsibility more than anything. Lexus Stagg was a young mother who had no business driving a car, never mind taking care of three children. For some reason, this 26-year-old mother thought that forcing her children to play chicken with a 2006 Lincoln Navigator was a good idea.

"You should be playing peekaboo with a 3-year-old instead of forcing him to try and dodge a 5,600 deadly weapon," said Sean Teare, chief of the Harris County District Attorney Office's vehicular crimes division. The situation is one that may seem inexplicable to most people, but it was captured on video just as Chief Teare said.

On the afternoon of June 11, 2019, Lexus Stagg left her apartment with her three children. The video shows that Stagg got into the vehicle alone and backed up quickly with the three children giving chase. She then drove forward quickly toward the children, causing them to jump out of the way. But not all of Stagg's children were able to get out of the way.

Three-year-old Lord Renfro Stagg was just too small and slow to get out of the way of the charging SUV. He fell under the vehicle's wheels and died instantly. The ensuing investigation revealed that not only could Renfro's death have been avoided, but also that Lexus Stagg put all of her children in danger numerous times with her game of chicken. It was a game that she always won, until the day her youngest child lost.

Some People Should Never Have Children

You've no doubt heard the phrase uttered, "Some people should never have children," or perhaps said it yourself. It's true, but unfortunately, the people who should never have children usually have the most. These children usually grow up in poverty, are surrounded by crime, and have parents who are negligent or abusive. Lexus Stagg was the poster girl for people who should never have children, so of course, she brought three into the world that she couldn't handle.

Since Stagg's case is ongoing, many of the details about her background haven't yet surfaced. Those that have are somewhat shocking. Stagg lived in west Houston her whole life, which is where she was living on June 11, 2019. She had two children before Lord was born in 2016 but records indicate that she did a lousy job raising them as well.

The Harris County Child Protective Services took the two children away in 2013, for reasons that are still unclear. Neighbors have told reporters that she was rarely home and left her children to fend for themselves. "I felt bad because those parents, they were never there, they were kind of negligent," said neighbor Walter Turcios.

Stagg's two older children were sent to live with relatives for a while, but as happens so often in these cases around the United States, they were eventually given back to their mother. There is no evidence that Stagg particularly liked being a mother or had any type of real affection for her children, but not having your children in the home means that any government assistance money you may be getting could come to an end.

As irresponsible as Stagg was with her first two children, she did the most irresponsible thing imaginable by having another child in 2016. The third time was not a charm—not for Lord nor for Stagg.

The Deadly Game

Based on police reports and interviews with Stagg's neighbors, Stagg liked to play a dangerous game of chicken with her children. If you are unfamiliar with the game of chicken, it usually involves two people driving their cars at each other; the first one to veer away is "chicken."

There are different variations of the game, which is apparently what Stagg liked to play with her children. In Stagg's version, only the children could ever be "chicken." She would back her vehicle up quickly, then the children would gather in front of the car. She would then drive forward real fast and they would usually jump out of the way. If you're wondering what the point of this "game" was, you are not alone. There doesn't seem to be one other than as a source of amusement for Stagg.

June 11, 2019 was a typical warm, muggy evening in Houston. It was 7:00 p.m. and Stagg was planning to take her children out for some fast food and to run some errands; but before they left, there was their normal routine of playing chicken.

Everything began just as it had countless times before, but when the children were supposed to jump out of the way, Stagg only saw her two oldest kids jumping off to the side. Lord was nowhere to be seen. As the kids were jumping out of the way, Lord must have tripped because he fell under the right front tire of the SUV.

Although Stagg ran over Lord, the front tire probably wasn't what killed him. After running over Lord with the front tire, Stagg either panicked or didn't realize she had just run over her kid, and just kept going, running over Lord's head with her back tire. Needless to say, Lord died at the scene.

An Attempted Coverup

Neighbors who witnessed the accident quickly came out of their apartments to lend a hand and within minutes police and ambulances were on the scene. Stagg told the responding officers that Lord had been killed when she was backing out and that she thought she hit a speed bump. She then said it was "an unfortunate accident."

But the police immediately thought it was strange. If Stagg were going to run errands with her children as she claimed, why weren't they in the car with her? It also didn't seem to make sense that the accident happened in the middle of the parking lot and that Stagg seemed more concerned about what was going to happen to her car than what had just happened to her son. The police took Stagg's statement and told her she was free to leave.

In the next several days, both the police and Stagg were busy. The detective interviewed Stagg's neighbors and learned that she wasn't such a great mother. Although they weren't surprised by the revelation, it seemed to confirm their suspicions that there was more to Lord's death than a simple accident.

Stagg was also busy. She immediately went on her social media accounts to elicit sympathy and to ostensibly give herself an alibi. Stagg repeated what she told the police—that it was an "accident"—and that she was badly hurting. In a long, rambling, poorly-written tribute she made to her son on Facebook, Stagg wrote, "Go What Do I Tell My 5 Year Old Daughter Who Witnessed Her Brothers Death."

As much as Stagg claimed she backed over her son in an accident, security camera footage from the apartment complex proved otherwise. Two weeks after she killed her son, Lexus Stagg was charged with criminally negligent homicide in his death. Although Stagg faces up to ten years in prison if convicted, it is a far cry from second-degree murder, which many in the Houston area believe she should be facing. The true insult came when Stagg went to her first court appearance.

As is customary in most American states, a defendant facing felony charges who is being held in jail usually goes before a judge within days of being charged for a bail hearing. Harris County prosecutors requested a $50,000 bond for Stagg, which would have been commensurate to what other defendants facing similar charges usually get. Even if a bondsman covered 90% of the bail, it still would've been too much for Stagg, effectively keeping her in jail until trial or a plea deal was reached.

But the judge had other ideas. For some reason, the judge set Stagg's bail at the unusually low amount of $1,500, an amount usually reserved for misdemeanors. Once the local media picked up the case, the public became incensed over the judge's low bail. Three days after issuing the low bail, the judge called Stagg back into court with somewhat of a compromise bond of $25,000. Lexus Stagg is currently sitting in the Harris County Jail awaiting trial.

CHAPTER 12

A "CARJACKER" DID IT, SUSAN SMITH

Many of you reading this probably remember the next case or at least some of the media spectacle that surrounded it. Depending upon which way you look at it, it all began—or came to a head—on October 25, 1994, when a 23-year-old South Carolina mother told police that she had just been carjacked and that her 3-year-old and 14-month-old sons were still in the car.

A very generic description of a black man wearing a stocking hat was given. The details of the where and how the carjacking took place were also cloudy. Still, the mother gave press conferences with her husband, the children's father, where she cried profusely, exhorting the supposed kidnapper to release her children.

America was gripped in fascination and horror with the case. The mother seemed so credible and sympathetic; after all, crime was a problem that more and more people were being affected by in the 1990s. But the police were not so certain of the mother's story. The details kept changing and the entire idea of a random carjacking-murder, although possible, seemed implausible in that particular community at the time.

Finally, after intense police pressure, the woman confessed to dumping the car in a lake with her children in it. Some of you may know that that woman is Susan Smith, but chances are you don't know the entire story.

The shocking case began long before Smith killed her children and blamed it on a specter and for several reasons, it continues to be a story today. There is no way to excuse what Susan Smith did, yet an examination of her life shows her to be somewhat sympathetic. It is not at all surprising that things happened the way they did. And perhaps just as interesting is the way chapters in this story continue to be written.

Susan Lee Vaughn

Susan Smith was born Susan Lee Vaughn to Harry and Linda Vaughn on September 26, 1971, near Greenville, South Carolina. Although Susan was born into a middle-class family, it was a less than ideal situation for a child. As with many young couples, Susan's parent's fought over money—Linda thought Harry didn't make enough of it.

Little is known about Harry, although there is some evidence that he suffered from mental illness. He would often be withdrawn and went through bouts of heavy drinking. Linda's nagging no doubt played a role in his mental state and there is also evidence that she cheated on him.

By late 1977, Harry had enough; he filed for divorce and left the family home. Susan was 6 years old when her father left, which is difficult enough for a child that age to deal with, but what happened next was devastating. Once the divorce was final, Harry killed himself.

The news confused and devastated Susan. Children that age are only starting to become self-aware and realize that life will someday end, so it is psychologically shattering when they see that firsthand with a parent.

But Linda had no problem quickly moving on with her life. Linda remarried a man named Beverly Russell just weeks after she divorced Harry, which raised more than a few eyebrows in conservative South Carolina and seemed to confirm the rumors that she was a cheater. With her father dead, Susan had a new father figure in her life who was quite different from Harry.

Beverly was an ultra-conservative fundamentalist Christian who made his new family attend services regularly and made the Bible the cornerstone of the Russell home. He made sure that the women of the house dressed conservatively and he was fairly domineering when it came to who Susan befriended. He claimed that everything he did was for their own good and to save them from eternal damnation, but by the time Susan was a teenager, Beverly's hypocrisy became evident.

Beverly used his domineering manner to seduce and sexually abuse Susan when she became a teenager. This claim was made not just by Susan, but by others who knew the Russell family. Susan reported the sexual abuse to her mother, who didn't believe her. For whatever reason, Linda decided that either Susan was lying or that the accusations were not serious enough to potentially ruin her marriage and the comfortable life Beverly gave her.

Susan also reported the abuse to the county social services, who did look into the case. Beverly moved out of the home for a few months, but when he realized that the county was not following up, he moved back and the sexual abuse began again.

Susan never filed another sexual abuse report with the county. Some people who knew Susan point to this period in her life as defining. She was exploited by her stepfather, her mother failed to protect her, and the local government authorities also failed to help. Susan learned that she couldn't count on anyone in life except herself. She also learned that sex can be used as a tool—a weapon—to get what one wants. Finally, Susan learned not to be sentimental and to move on quickly.

A Good Façade

Despite the turmoil that was unfolding in Susan's homelife during her teen years, her school life was quite the opposite. She learned quickly to keep her problems to herself and rarely told friends or teachers what was taking place at home. In school, Susan was popular and active in extra-curricular activities. She was voted president of the Junior Civitan Club in her junior year, which was a student organization that volunteered in the community. She came up with many of the group's activities and was always one of the first members to come forward when it was time to volunteer. Susan was also voted the "friendliest female" her senior year.

But all of that was just a façade to hide her true feelings or lack thereof. Although Susan was popular and got along well with all of her fellow students and teachers, few people *knew* her in high school. She generally didn't let many people get very close and when she did it was on a superficial level, often sexually.

Thanks to her stepfather, Susan Vaughn became sexually active before most of her classmates in conservative 1980s South Carolina. During the summer of 1988, when she was between her junior and senior years of high school, Susan took a job as a bookkeeper at a local Winn-Dixie supermarket. Susan was good with numbers and showed a lot of promise in the job. She also got along well with her fellow employees. Especially the male employees.

Susan had already been sexually active for a few years with her stepfather when she took the job at Winn-Dixie, but an older married man who worked there caught her eye. The two began an illicit affair and although she liked the man, he just viewed the relationship as a fling. Possibly to make the older man jealous, Susan also began having sex with a high school student who worked at the store.

The ploy of course didn't get the guy to leave his wife, but it did mark the beginning of a pattern that Susan would follow throughout her life, eventually leading her to murder. She used sex as a tool to get what she wanted and what she usually wanted was a married man.

All of the sexual activity Susan was engaging in finally caught up with her during her senior year of high school. When she learned that she was pregnant, she was faced with one of the biggest decisions in her life. Susan knew that, if she kept the baby, she would probably have to drop out of high school and it would also seriously cramp her lifestyle—she would probably have to move out of her mother's and stepfather's home. She also figured it would be difficult to attract an attractive man.

Then there was the problem of who the father was. She was having sex with two men at work in addition to Beverly when she got pregnant, so it could have been any of theirs. None of them were suitable partners: her stepfather, a high school kid, and a married man.

Faced with all of these problems, Susan decided to have an abortion. As with most of her other problems in life, Susan was able to keep her abortion a secret from most people, which only served to eat her up inside. She put on a cheerful face at school and work, but she was a wreck.

So, one day, Susan decided to take a bottle of Tylenol to end her pain. It is unknown if Susan's overdose was a legitimate suicide attempt or a cry for help. Most people who are trying to kill themselves usually don't use over the counter pain killers, but it may have been all that Susan had at her disposal.

While Susan was in the hospital recovering from the overdose, she told the doctors that she had previously attempted suicide similarly when she was 13 but she had kept it a secret. So Susan cleaned herself up and went back to her routine none the worse for wear or at least that was what those who knew about the overdose thought. She graduated from high school and began working at Winn-Dixie fulltime, looking for a way out of her life.

The Ides of March

David Smith was one of the eligible men Susan met at work. He was nice, average looking, a hard worker, and most importantly, he wasn't married. David and Susan were nearly the same age and had a similar background in fundamental Christianity, but they were otherwise fairly different.

David Smith was for the most part a "good boy." He didn't party much in high school and wasn't having sex with multiple partners during the same time frame as Susan was. He had heard rumors about Susan's past, but he didn't seem to care because that was all in the past.

David wanted to start a family, so he proposed to Susan and after she accepted they set the date for March 15, 1991—the "Ides of March." If you aren't familiar with the significance of the "Ides of March," don't feel bad. Unless you have a background in the Classics or are a big fan of Shakespeare's *Julius Caesar*, you wouldn't have a reason to know what it is. The Ides of March is simply March 15, but for the Roman dictator Julius Caesar, it was the day he was assassinated on the floor of the Senate in 44 BCE. In Shakespeare's version of the true story, Caesar had been warned to "beware the Ides of March." Of course, he didn't heed the warning and paid for it with his life.

In the centuries since Julius Caesar, the Ides of March has become a sort of catchphrase among the more erudite for a disastrous or potentially disastrous occasion. But David and Susan Smith weren't versed in the Classics or Shakespeare; the Bible was their book and according to it, they should have a family. So, the couple welcomed Michael Daniel into their family on October 10, 1991, and Alexander Tyler on August 5, 1993. David wanted to have more children, but problems within the home kept that from becoming a reality.

The Smiths were not unlike many young couples that have financial problems. Susan liked to spend more money than either of them were making, which alone caused problems between them, but her solution created even more fissures in the already cracking relationship. Susan often went to her mother for money, which David didn't like for a couple of reasons. First, there was the matter of pride. He knew that he made enough money to support his family and that it was just an issue of Susan getting her spending under control.

And then there was the matter of Linda. Besides finances, nosy in-laws are often cited as a major problem in marriages. Linda Russell was a domineering and nosy woman who wanted to control every aspect of Susan's life. Since Susan liked to spend money and have nice things, Linda used that as leverage to influence her daughter and insert herself more and more into the couple's life.

Needless to say, the money problems and mother-in-law meddling began to have a deleterious effect on the young marriage. David did what he could do to put Linda's money to good use by using some of it for a down payment on a home in November 1992 after Susan became pregnant with Alexander. But the house and the second child were just band-aids on the growing cancer that was the Smiths' marriage. Susan and David both had affairs, eventually separating for a few months in early 1993. They reunited for the birth of Alexander, but neither's hearts were really in the marriage at that point. They were both just going through the motions.

"You Have to Act Like a Nice Girl"

Despite her plethora of personal problems, Susan Smith was always a consummate professional in all of her jobs. She was regularly promoted and given raises based on her work ethic and performance. In 1993, she took a position as an executive secretary at Conso Products in Greenville. The position meant more responsibilities and pay, but most importantly, it introduced Susan to her next paramour—Tom Findlay.

Tom Findlay was not just another guy either; he was the son of J. Carey Findlay, the CEO of Conso Products. Findlay was an important and wealthy man, making him a target for Susan, and the fact that he was married didn't matter to her. It didn't matter much to him either.

Susan and Tom had an on-again/off-again relationship throughout most of 1994. The always duplicitous Susan was attempting to reconcile with David during the process while Tom was married and hiding the affair from his wife. Tom Findlay had no intention of ever leaving his wife and to his credit, he told Susan that on numerous occasions.

For whatever reason, though, be it true love or obsession, Susan kept pursuing Findlay. Susan even filled out divorced papers, and just as she was about to officially file them, she sent a letter to Findlay on October 17, 1994. She claimed that her marriage was over and that the two of them could now run away together.

For his part, Findlay was not interested in continuing the affair. He decided to reconcile with his wife and to quit seeing Susan. He told her as much in a detailed letter. In one part of the letter, he twisted the knife relating to Susan's promiscuous ways. "If you want to catch a nice guy like me one day, you have to act like a nice girl. And you know, nice girls don't sleep with married men," Findlay wrote.

The letter was a blow to Susan's plans, but she had one last card to play. Susan had learned at an early age how to use sex and her sexuality to her advantage, so she attempted to gain sympathy by telling Tom about the relationship she had with her stepfather. When that didn't work, Susan told Tom that she'd had sex with his father.

It remains unknown if that were the case. J. Carey would later deny the accusation, but Susan certainly did know how to seduce men and it wouldn't have been out of her playbook to do so in this situation. Regardless, this last ploy didn't work.

Yet Susan refused to accept that the affair was over. She kept thinking about what she could do to win Tom back and if there was something that she had done wrong. Then it came to her. She remembered that Tom didn't seem to care much for children. He had said that one of the reasons he didn't want to leave his wife for her was because he didn't want to take care of the Smith children.

The reality is that Tom probably just said that to get Susan to back off, but in her warped mind, she turned that into a reason to kill. Now, for Susan Smith, the only way she would have Tom Findlay is if she killed her children.

Susan's plan was very well thought out and the police quickly saw right through it. On the morning of October 25, 1994, Susan tried to speak with Tom one last time, but when he didn't return her call, she decided to go with "Plan B." That afternoon, Susan got her two sons, buckled them into their seats, and drove to John D. Long Lake. The lake is a popular recreational reservoir in Union County, but by the time Susan got there, it was evening and no one was around.

It was just as she wanted it. As her two sons were sleeping, Susan Smith got out of her car and let it roll into the lake. The first part of Plan B was accomplished, so now she had to move on to the next part. Susan ran to a nearby home and hysterically claimed that she had just been carjacked at a red light in town and was dropped off near the lake. She explained that her two young sons were still in the car, presumably with the carjacker, and that the police needed to be called.

Susan could've won an Oscar for her performance, or at least an Emmy, as it was very convincing to the responding officers. Since children were involved, though, they had to take everything very seriously, so a search was immediately conducted in the area. Nothing was found.

For Susan, her devious little plan immediately started paying off dividends. The crime brought Susan sympathy from her friends, family, and strangers from around the community and once the national media began reporting on it, people from all over the world began showing their sympathy for the mother and her two missing children.

For Susan, although the act may not have brought Tom running back into her arms, she got the consolation prize of David. Yes, David got back with Susan to help console his wife and the mother of his children, as well as to help with the investigation. David was also going through a lot of pain and thought that, despite his differences and problems with Susan, she would be a good pillar of support.

The couple gave interviews to the press where both were visibly upset, although, in retrospect, we now know that Susan was acting. "I just feel like my whole world's been taken away," said Susan in an interview while crying. "My children are my life and they just gotta be okay."

To most people, Susan's story seemed believable. Violent crime is a problem in many parts of the United States, which includes Union County, South Carolina and what reason would she have to make up such a story? And if you assumed that she made up the story, then that meant she was somehow involved in her children's disappearance. It was just a bridge too far for most people.

But it wasn't a bridge too far for the Union County Sheriff's Department. During Susan's first interview with the police, she told them that a generic-looking black guy wearing a stocking hat carjacked her while she was at a red light. When asked if there were any other cars at the light that may have seen the crime, Susan was emphatic that there weren't.

Besides actually killing her children, that was Susan Smith's first mistake. Sheriff Howard Mills knew that the traffic light that Susan claimed to have been carjacked at only turns red if there is another vehicle present, which meant that she was probably lying.

The inconsistency in Smith's story certainly didn't look good, but it wasn't enough to make an arrest or even to get a search warrant. It did tell Mills that he was on the right track in thinking that it wasn't some random carjacker who committed the crime. With that in mind, Mills requested Smith to come to the sheriff's department for another interview on November 30 to clear up a few things.

When Smith sat down in the interrogation room, there was no longer any "good cop, bad cop." It was Mills straight confronting Smith, telling her he knew she killed the boys and that she knows where they are. Susan began sobbing and asked Mills to pray with her.

After the two said a prayer, Smith told Mills the entire story. She claimed that she originally intended to die with her children but that she jumped out at the last minute. She told Mills exactly where she put the car into the lake, which was an area the sheriff's department had searched weeks earlier. The bodies of the Smith boys were found in the car along with the letter Tom sent to Susan.

Facing the Needle

When the news broke that Susan Smith had confessed to murdering her children, the nation was shocked. "How could a mother do that to her children?" people asked. It just wasn't conceivable to most people, especially when some of the details of why she did it began to be publicized.

As the weeks went on, the shock was quickly replaced with anger. Most people in Union County, South Carolina were angry that Smith had taken advantage of their goodwill and others were upset that her accusations caused racial tension in the area that has a history of racial problems. Activist Jesse Jackson made numerous appearances on television, speaking about how Susan Smith's black carjacker meme had hurt his community.

But all of that was noise in the background to Susan Smith. She was facing the death penalty for her crimes in a state where people are regularly executed by lethal injection. Smith had no plea bargains offered to her and had little defense. Since the prosecution didn't offer a plea bargain and pursued the death penalty, it meant that Smith would have to come up with some type of defense. Her lawyers had their work cut out for them.

Smith's attorneys knew that, with the mountain of physical evidence against their client, and more importantly her confession, the best they could do was to keep her off death row. To do that, they focused on the abuse Susan suffered throughout her early life. Several credible witnesses were called to testify to the fact that Susan was abused by her stepfather, which seemed to elicit a certain amount of sympathy, or pity, from those in attendance in the courtroom. It also helped that Smith appeared catatonic during the trial and started sobbing whenever her children were mentioned.

On the other side, the prosecution depicted Smith as a selfish, manipulative, cold-blooded killer, who saw her children as standing in the way of her happiness. As far as high profile, first-degree murder trials are concerned, Susan Smith's trial moved very quickly. The verdict was announced in July 1995—guilty on both counts of first-degree murder. Of course, the verdict was no surprise to anyone familiar with the case, so the question became: what would her sentence be, life or death?

The defense's strategy paid off because, in the end, the jury spared Smith's life. She was handed a life sentence, which in South Carolina means that she must serve a minimum of 30 years behind bars. Smith will be eligible for parole in 2024.

Most people thought that was the last they'd hear from Susan Smith and that, if karma had anything to do with it, then she would be living a miserable life behind bars. But karma is a complicated thing.

Some Things Don't Change

Susan was sent to do her time in the Camille Griffin Graham Correctional Institution in Columbia, South Carolina. The prison is the main and most secure women's prison in the state—with the amount of time she had to do and the high profile nature of her case, there was no way Susan was going to do her time in a lower security camp. Susan spent her first few years in relative isolation from most of the other inmate population who wanted her dead.

David divorced her and only her closest family members kept in contact. Eventually, Susan fell into prison life and eventually back into some of her old habits and lifestyles. A review of Smith's record behind bars reveals that she brought many of her problems and proclivities with her to Graham. She was written up on more than one occasion for self-mutilation and was busted for possessing illicit drugs, but perhaps the most interesting details of her incarceration involve her sexual activity.

It is unknown at this point if Smith has been sexually involved with any of her fellow inmates, but she was having sex with at least two different guards. Once the affairs became known, the guards were arrested and charged with felonies. Susan was transferred to another prison, in what can only be described as a not-so-unexpected situation. It was also revealed that Susan contracted a venereal disease at Camille Griffin Graham.

Susan has had little contact with the media but wrote a letter in 2015 to Harrison Cahill, a reporter for the local Union County newspaper *The State*. In the letter, Susan was adamant that she was not a bad person, writing "I am not the monster society thinks I am. I am far from it." Most people would beg to differ.

CHAPTER 13

DIANE STAUDTE AND THE SWEET TASTE OF DEATH

Parents will never admit that they sometimes play favorites with their children. Nearly every person who has siblings has thought about this at one point in their life, whether or not it is true, and some have seen the outright bias at work. Most of the time, the favoritism is fairly minor and barely recognizable. One of the children may be a higher achiever and is regularly praised, while the other children in the family may find it a bit harder to please their parents.

In some families, the favoritism is a bit more apparent. Some parents come right out and tell their children which ones they favor. Doing such a thing is cruel and tends to create low self-esteem in the children not favored, as well as unnecessary competition among the children.

But Diane Staudte took the favoritism of some of her children to a level of evil that has been rarely seen in even the most dysfunctional families. Over a year, Diane killed her husband, son, and almost killed one of her daughters in a twisted plot to claim a relatively small amount of life insurance. Staudte slowly poisoned her family members' Gatorade and other sweet drinks, giving them slow, painful deaths that most people would never want to see their worst enemies endure.

As twisted as it was that Diane Staudte attempted to wipe out her family, that alone would not make this case unique among all of these cases of motherly murder. No, what makes Diane Staudte's case unique is that she played extreme favorites among her children by not only saving one of her daughters from her diabolical plan but also enlisting her help. And the daughter went along with her mom's plan. Needless to say, there won't be many family reunions in the Staudte family.

The Staudtes

To anyone who knew the Staudte family in the late 1990s to the early 2010s, they seemed like the most average, normal American family you could meet. They lived in one of the most middle American cities in the country—Springfield, Missouri—in a middle income, working-class neighborhood. Husband Mark Staudte was described by all who knew him as a hardworking but fun-loving guy. When he wasn't working to put food on the table for his family, he was playing in a blues band that did gigs in local bars.

Wife Diane was known as a caring woman and a pillar in the community. She too was musically inclined, playing the organ at her Lutheran church for over 30 years. The couple had three children: Rachel was the oldest, Shaun was the middle child, and Sarah was the youngest. By all accounts, the family seemed to genuinely care for each other and got along well, but there were favorites. Mark was not said to have favorites among his children, although Diane made it clear which child she preferred—Rachel.

"They were close," said Mark's best friend and fellow bandmate, Rob Mancuso, about Diane and Rachel. The mother and daughter spent a lot of time together, often excluding the others in the family. They would spend hours together shopping, watching television, and even taking trips. Mark and the other Staudte children didn't seem to mind that they were so close; Shaun had problems of his own and Sarah was busy with college by the time the two became deadly close. Yet it was a relationship that should have sent warning signals up to all who knew them. It went far beyond simple favoritism and into the realm of evil manipulation.

Murder Never Tasted So Sweet

Despite her appearance as a family-orientated church-going lady, Diane Staudte was a self-centered, greedy woman. She was always looking for ways to improve her economic and social standing, even if it meant cutting moral, ethical, and legal corners. For the most part, though, Diane's activities in that regard were relatively tame until late 2011.

Around late 2011, Diane began thinking of a way to get rid of her husband, whom she was growing tired of but didn't want to divorce. She reasoned that a divorce could be long, and in the end, she really wouldn't get much. If she killed Mark, though, she could stand to get a life insurance settlement. Mark only had a $20,000 policy on his life, but Diane figured that it was enough to give her and Rachel a new start. Diane wasn't planning on sharing any of her ill-gotten gains with her other children because they too would be dead!

Diane brought the plan to Rachel in the fall of 2011 and she agreed that it seemed like a good idea. Diane was generally tired of Mark and she reasoned that, due to his health problems, there probably wouldn't be much of an investigation. As evil as the plot to kill Mark may have been, the reasons for killing Shaun and Sarah were even harder to grasp.

Shaun suffered from autism, which left him developmentally disabled and unable to properly function in society. Although he was 25 years old in 2011, he still lived at home and didn't work. Mark genuinely cared for Shaun and had no problem with him living at home, but Diane resented the resources and attention he required. She saw him as a pest that needed to be eliminated.

Diane also viewed his youngest daughter, Sarah, as a pest but for slightly different reasons. Sarah had recently graduated from college and had moved back home while she looked for a fulltime job and paid off some of her college loan debts. Sarah wasn't much different than many young Americans in that respect, but Diane felt she was a burden. So Diane decided that she would kill Mark, Shaun, and Sarah. And Rachel was willing to go along with the whole plan.

Like many female killers throughout history, particularly black widows, the pair decided that they were going to poison their family. They knew that antifreeze was a deadly poison that could be administered slowly over months, but due to it being used in murders, most manufacturers had changed the ingredients so that it had a bitter, not a sweet taste. After doing a little investigative work, the two found that they could buy some sweet-tasting antifreeze on the Internet.

Diane and Rachel believed their plan was foolproof—they would add one or two teaspoons to their victims' sweet-tasting drinks, such as soda and Gatorade, and then watch them deteriorate. It would be an effective, yet slow and agonizing method to kill their victims.

Mark was the first victim to succumb to Diane and Rachel's sweet-tasting death. He showed no signs of poisoning for months until he suddenly had flu-like symptoms just before Easter 2012. Since Mark thought that he had the flu, he did what most people do and stayed home, got some rest, and drank plenty of fluids. The problem was, those fluids were laced with antifreeze.

Mark died on Easter Day 2012 at the age of 61. The doctor who examined his body noticed a discolored ring around his mouth but thought little of it. The doctor also didn't think much of Mark's age or manner of death. Plenty of people died in their sixties and Mark was not in very good health: he was overweight, drank too much, and had several health ailments. The death was ruled natural.

Diane then moved into phase two of her plan by having Mark cremated. Once the body was gone, there was virtually no way she could get caught; all she had to do then was claim the life insurance policy. The insurance company didn't give Diane any problems, and within a couple of months, she was able to claim the money, which allowed her to move into a nicer house in a better neighborhood. Still, she had two other problems to take care of first!

The devious mother-daughter duo turned their attention to Shaun, putting small amounts of antifreeze into his sports drinks and sodas daily. About five months after Mark died, their poisoning finally paid off when Shaun died with flu-like symptoms. One would think that since Shaun was only 26 and since his father died in similarly only months earlier, that someone would've investigated his death; but no investigation happened. The doctor even noticed a similar ring around Shaun's mouth, but since he had several health problems, which included a history of seizures, his death was also ruled natural.

Diane and Rachel went back to their new home in the suburbs and began planning their last kill. Sarah was their next victim, but since she was younger and in better health, she proved to be difficult to kill. The pair began poisoning her in late 2012 and by the summer of 2013, the plan had almost worked. In June 2013, Sarah checked herself into an emergency room at a local hospital with flu-like symptoms. The doctors thought it was suspicious that a seemingly healthy 24-year old would be so ill, so they kept her in the hospital for treatment.

Although Sarah survived the ordeal, she was left with permanent neurological problems. The doctors were at a loss to diagnose her illness, but then an unlikely person came forward with some interesting information. The Staudte's family minister told the doctors about the deaths of Mark and Shaun, which led them to believe that Sarah had been poisoned. Tests were run on Sarah that showed signs of poisoning, so the Springfield Police were called. The police knew that poisoning cases almost always happen within the home.

Arrests and Trials

Once it was determined that Sarah had been poisoned and that her father and brother had died under what were later determined to be suspicious circumstances, things moved very quickly. Detective Neil McAmis led the investigation, knowing that the answer was with Diane.

Diane agreed to come into the police station without a lawyer present and at first denied having anything to do with any poisoning. But McAmis kept at her, calling her a liar and pointing out that almost all poisonings happen within the home. Finally, Diane admitted to the crimes but refused to take complete responsibility.

Diane took the route that many people do when the evidence of their guilt is clear—she blamed her crimes on the victims. She said that Mark was abusive and that she feared for her life, but when McAmis asked what that had to do with Shaun and Sarah, she had no defense. But she did explain in Shaun's case. "Shaun would be interfering with whatever I would do," Diane told McAmis. "He was more than a bother...more than a pest."

As bad as that sounds, Staudte then added an equally bizarre statement. "I'm not a perpetual killer. I'm just stupid." Although not many people would probably argue with Diane Staudte over her lack of intelligence, her "perpetual killer" statement is interesting, to say the least. She more than likely meant "serial killer." If that is the case, then she wasn't technically a serial killer because she only killed two people. Though, if she'd had it her way, there would have been three victims.

Eventually, there may have been four. There is no reason that Rachel wouldn't have been her next victim at some point down the road. Diane Staudte was a very violent and greedy person who thought nothing of killing her family members for some material comfort. Rachel may have been lucky being her mother's favorite for a time, but Diane had no problem throwing her favorite child under the bus when she was arrested.

It didn't take Rachel long to confess to the whole plot. She began singing to detective McAmis as soon as she got into the interrogation room and she revealed many more details of the plan. When the police conducted a search warrant of the Staudte home, they uncovered even more damning evidence. Some of the special sweet-tasting antifreeze was discovered but even worse for the mother-daughter duo was Rachel's diary, which admitted to and detailed the murder plot.

One entry stated, "It's sad when I realized how my father will pass on in the next two months...Shaun, my brother will move on shortly after...It will be tough getting used to the changes but everything will work out." The entry was dated June 13, 2011, which proved premeditation and the fact that it was a long-term plot.

Like her mother, Rachel tried to mitigate her guilt to a certain extent. Rachel claimed that she tried to talk her mother out of poisoning Shaun and Sarah, by telling her that they should put Shaun in some type of group home. She also warned Sarah that she had to leave. In the end, though, when her mother didn't agree, she ended up going along with the plan.

Finally, Rachel told McAmis why each member of the Staudte family was murdered. "As far as Dad, it was for a little peace." "Shaun, because he was annoying." "Sarah was just nosy. Very nosy." Rachel never corroborated her mother's allegations of abuse. Diane was simply tired of her husband and two of her three children.

Both women were charged with two counts of first-degree murder and faced the prospect of either spending the rest of their lives in prison or the death penalty. In Missouri, the death penalty is regularly handed out and carried through more often than in most states. The women were denied bail and held in the Greene County Jail in Springfield for trial.

While Rachel was awaiting trial in jail, she had a lot of time to contemplate her situation. She had followed her orders without question and now found herself facing a potential death sentence. The prosecution believed that Diane manipulated and led Rachel into

131

committing these horrible crimes, but the reality was that there was more evidence against her than her mother. So the prosecution decided to offer Rachel a deal. They would allow her to plead guilty to one count of second-degree murder in return for testifying against her mother at her trial. Rachel agreed and pled guilty in May 2015, but sentencing was withheld until Diane's trial was concluded.

Diane had no way out of her situation. She had gone too far trying to poison Sarah, and since that time, the house of cards that was her life quickly came crashing down. Diane's attorneys went through the motions of preparing for her defense but had no real arguments on her behalf. Even if they could somehow paint Mark as an abusive husband, it couldn't explain why Shaun was murdered or why Sarah was nearly killed.

So, to avoid a costly, lengthy trial, the prosecution allowed Diane to plead guilty to one count of first-degree murder in exchange for dropping the death penalty. Diane Staudte pled guilty to first-degree murder in January 2016 and was sentenced to life without parole.

Rachel was then sentenced in March 2016. Although her testimony against Diane was not ultimately required, her agreement to testify was taken into consideration. She was given a lengthy prison sentence whereby she will have to serve at least 42 years before she is considered for parole. Since Rachel was 25 when she was sentenced, she will be an old woman if she is ever released. Needless to say, Sarah doesn't have any plans to see her mother or sister on visiting day.

CHAPTER 14

THE DEVIL MADE HER DO IT, ISABEL MARTINEZ

For most people, the phrase, "the Devil made me do it" is more metaphorical than anything. Although most people believe in good and evil and many believe in the presence of Satan, few think that the Dark One can directly influence our day-to-day lives.

We don't hear the Devil talking to us, and if we do, then most would probably think it's time to check into a mental health facility. But there are some among us who honestly believe that we are little more than marionettes being played by higher forces, good and evil. Of course, many of the people who believe this suffer from delusions and mental illness, which is the case of Isabel Martinez.

On July 6, 2017, Isabel Martinez was a 33-year-old mother of five living in suburban Atlanta. She was an illegal alien living on the legal fringes of society, but more importantly, she suffered from strange delusions that placed her on the fringes of sanity. Isabel Martinez thought that the Devil was guiding her to commit unspeakable acts of violence. She claims that Satan and his minions repeatedly told her to murder people, especially members of her family, which would be the only way she'd ever find peace.

Finally, on the early morning hours of July 6, 2017, Martinez gave in to the wishes of the Dark Lord and committed one of the worst prolicides in the history of the state of Georgia. The massacre left four of

Martinez's children and her husband dead and the community asking many questions. After Martinez was arrested and brought to court, her antics in the courtroom made many think that she truly was insane, but others are skeptical, thinking that she is merely playing the system.

The Romero Family

Not much is known about Maria Isabel Garduno-Martinez other than she is a Mexican national who entered the United States illegally sometime in the 2000s. According to Immigration and Customs Enforcement (ICE), Martinez had been living in Georgia for about 12 years before the massacre, but it is unknown if she had lived in another U.S. state before that or for how long.

It also isn't known how long she was with her common-law husband Martin Romero, who was 33 at the time of the murders. Romero was also a Mexican national in the United States illegally. What is known about Martinez is that she is not a particularly attractive woman. She is short, overweight, and has a curious-looking receding hairline. As physically unattractive as Martinez may be, she also looks rather unassuming and unimposing. Isabel Martinez doesn't look like she is capable of murdering an entire family.

Isabel and her family were living in the suburban Atlanta town of Loganville, which is in Gwinnet County. Gwinnet County, in general, and Loganville specifically, have changed quite a bit demographically in the last 20 years. The county went from having a small Hispanic population to majority Hispanic in many of its towns and neighborhoods. Most of the Hispanics in Gwinnet County are from Mexico and other Central American countries and many of them are in the United States illegally.

It was the perfect place for Isabel and her husband to lie low and blend into their surroundings. The Romero children went to local schools and began learning English, but spoke Spanish exclusively at home. Their primarily Hispanic neighbors said that the Romeros were friendly but primarily kept to themselves. The parents worked and when home spent most of their time inside. The Romero children played with the other kids in the neighborhood and weren't a problem for adults or children. The Romeros built a somewhat stable life on the fringes of American society, but there were signs that something was wrong.

Isabel seemed to take some religious ideas to heart and began claiming that evil spirits were hovering all around her, trying to make her commit evil acts. The situation seemed to get worse when the family took a vacation to Savannah, Georgia. Isabel stood calmly watching the waters of the Atlantic Ocean and when her family asked why she was so interested in the water, she replied that she believed the waves were evil and were trying to take her children. The trip was a portent of worse things to come.

The Loganville Massacre

The evening of July 5 went like any other in the Romero house. Since it was the summer, the kids stayed up a little later, but by 10:00 p.m. all of them were asleep: 10-year-old Isabela Martinez, 9-year-old Diana Romero, 7-year-old Dacota Romero, 4-year-old Dillan Romero, and 2-year-old Alex Romero. The parents also went to sleep, but sometime after midnight, Isabel awoke from her slumber.

Her demons were calling her to carry out the evil act. Isabel took a knife out of the kitchen, quietly walked over to where her children were sleeping, and methodically began stabbing at them. The children began screaming and crying when they realized what was happening, but most of them were too small and scared to fight off their mother's frenzied attack.

Martin woke up to the massacre and tried to grab the knife from his wife, but she stabbed in him the arms and when he instinctively pulled back she stabbed in vital areas. He fell to the ground, slowly bleeding to death. Isabel then turned her attention back to her children. One by one, she stabbed her children in their necks and bodies, making sure that they would never take another breath of life on this Earth.

When she got to Diana, she told her daughter the motive for the attack. You are "going to the sky to see Jesus," she told Diana before attacking. The frenzied attack was over within a matter of minutes, but there were still a couple of things that Isabel had to do. The short but stout mother dragged all of the bodies, including her husband's, into the same room so that "everyone could be together," as she later said. Martinez then called the police around 5:00 a.m. to report the crime.

The Devil Made Me Do It

When the police showed up at the Romero home, they were shocked at the level of carnage. The responding officers didn't think that the short, squat woman in front of them could do such damage, which is why they were inclined to believe her when she said that a family friend committed the atrocity. But of course, that just didn't add up. If a family friend had killed all of the Romeros, why did they let Isabel live?

The police also noticed that Isabel had what appeared to be some cuts on her hands. So, they brought her into the Gwinnett County Sheriff's Department for questioning, and eventually they realized she was the killer. Isabel Martinez was arrested on five counts of murder that afternoon.

Once Diana Romero recovered from her injuries, she gave a complete statement against her mother, which provided undeniable proof of her guilt, but possibly also her insanity. Martinez then met with county social workers, telling them that the devil made her commit the murders. She further explained that the murders were the culmination of a demonic possession that began months earlier when she went to the ocean with her family.

The Gwinnet County prosecutors were not so convinced that Martinez was crazy. They pointed to the fact that she initially tried to blame the

136

murders on a neighbor and also noted that she had no known history of mental illness. The entire story just seemed too "tight" to them. But would a sane person brutally murder five members of her family?

When Martinez appeared at her first hearing, she did act crazy. She smiled for the camera, giving the "thumbs up" sign on one occasion. Martinez's behavior caused a legal conundrum for the prosecution: if they pursued and got the death penalty as much of the public wanted, it could be overturned on appeal due to her mental state.

Because of the legal considerations, the Gwinnet County prosecutors took the death penalty off the table as long as Martinez would plead guilty to first-degree murder and accept a sentence of life in prison with no chance of parole. Martinez agreed to the plea bargain in April 2019 and was promptly shipped off to her new home in the Georgia Department of Corrections. If Martinez's craziness was all an act, it may have saved her life.

CHAPTER 15

KILLING FOR THE APOCALYPSE, DENA SCHLOSSER

The next case is perhaps the strangest and most brutal of all the cases in this anthology. Although the murdering mom involved *only* killed one of her children, she did so in such a horrific manner and for such a strange motive that it stands out. Dena Schlosser was a very religious woman who believed that the world was in its final days. It's not quite clear how she came to that realization, but at some point, she began believing that we were on the verge of the Biblical Apocalypse.

Believing in the impending Biblical Apocalypse is not necessarily strange, especially in the American Bible Belt, and preparing for the Apocalypse is not strange either. Many true believers carefully study scripture to find clues as to what is coming next and what they believe they should do. They study every word of the Book of Revelation and compare it with Old Testament prophecy books, such as Daniel and Ezekiel, for answers. These people often meet with and share their opinions with other like-minded people. They sometimes try to convince others that they need to "get right with God" before the Apocalypse, which could happen at any minute.

Then there are some who physically prepare for the end in addition to their spiritual preparations. With The Bible in one hand and an AK-47 in the other, some people believe that the Book of Revelation warns of impending social collapse and widespread war. These people believe that, when the impending Apocalypse takes they need to be on the right side, not only spiritually but also physically.

Then there is Dena Schlosser. Dena Schlosser believed that the Biblical Apocalypse was upon us and she also believed that there were things she needed to do to face it. But instead of Bible study or even prepping, Schlosser thought that amputating the arms of her 11-month daughter was the best course of action. Yes, you read that correctly!

The case raised many questions, not so much about Schlosser's guilt, but more so about her state of mind. A sane person wouldn't do such a thing to her child and for the reason stated, right? The case brought to the forefront questions about mental illness and how mentally ill people charged with crimes should be treated in the criminal justice system.

Long after the final judgment was made in the courtroom, this case continued for several years and still does in many ways. In a macabre bit of irony, this case even eventually intersected with the Andrea Yates case, proving that the world of matronly murderesses is truly a small one.

Early Difficulties

Dena Schlosser was born Dena Laettner in 1969 in upstate New York. Although she was born into a quiet, middle-class family, she had some afflictions that made her early life more difficult and may have contributed to the later tragedy.

Dena was born with the condition hydrocephalus. As the name indicates, it is a medical condition where the newborn has excessive fluid around the brain, which can lead to severe problems, but is very treatable. A child suffering from hydrocephalus will have a larger than average head until the excess fluid is drained, either through surgery or other treatments, and the growth of the body can then catch up with the head.

Children can be cruel, as Dena found out growing up with hydrocephalus. She was teased for having a "potato head" and for being bald. Although hair loss is not a side effect of hydrocephalus, Dena had eight surgeries before the age of 13 to eliminate the fluid, which meant that her head needed to be shaved.

So, childhood was not easy for Dena Laettner, but she persevered as well as she could. She spent a lot of time at home with her family, reading, and doing her homework. Dena also became interested in the Bible at a young age, often reading scriptures in her free time. Dena's diligent work and study habits paid off when she graduated. She applied to several universities in the region and was accepted into the exclusive Marist College. Located in Poughkeepsie, New York, it offered the two primary factors she was seeking in a college: it was close to home and it had an excellent academic reputation.

Taking her study habits and work ethic she developed in high school with her to college, Dena was a good student, earning a degree in psychology in four years. Dena's social life in college was also somewhat similar to that of her high school years—she focused on her grades and had little time for the party scene. She did, though, take the time to dive deeper into The Bible, which is how she met John Schlosser.

John Schlosser was a fellow Marist student when Dena met him in the mid-1980s. The two were immediately attracted to each other, but more importantly, they shared similar morals. John and Dena were both ardent Christians and often spent much of their free time together, reading scripture and discussing Biblical passages.

Although John didn't graduate from college, he was always able to land well-paying jobs, so he made the next logical step any good Christian would do and asked Dena to marry him. She accepted and within months they had moved to the suburbs of Dallas, Texas. The move was primarily based on the fact that John would have better career opportunities in Texas to make more money for their desired large family. Although Dena was the one in the family with a college background, John didn't want her working. Dena would be a good Christian mother and stay home and raise their children.

Life Before the Apocalypse

The Schlossers moved to the nice, quiet Dallas suburb of Plano, Texas, and began building a life according to their Christian beliefs. Dena gave birth to a daughter in 1995 and another in 1998, and by all accounts, she was happy being a mother. John worked and she was a full-time mother.

Everything seemed to be going well for the young family. They were well respected by their neighbors and fellow church members and appeared to be upwardly-mobile socially and economically. John was doing so well at his job that the couple decided to have another child. Although they were hoping for a boy, they were happy to welcome their third daughter, Margaret, into their family in December 2003.

As soon as Margaret was born, though, Dena's mental state quickly unraveled. The day after Margaret was born, Dena attempted suicide. It is unclear if the suicide attempt was a "cry for help" or a legitimate attempt to take her own life, but either way, it probably should have been taken more seriously. There were no efforts made to get Dena any mental health counseling or any type of treatment.

The birth of Margaret was an enormous burden for Dena to deal with and it was also difficult for John. He did what he could do to help with the children to alleviate his wife's mental state, but he couldn't afford to take much time off work. And, unfortunately for the Schlossers, they had no immediate family in the area. There were no parents or siblings who could help watch the children.

A couple of weeks after Dena attempted suicide, the county child protective services were called to the family home over another bizarre incident. Dena was reportedly running down the street, with her 5-year-old child giving chase on her bike. When the police and social workers arrived at the home, they found out that Dena had begun acting bizarre and had suddenly run out of the house and down the street, which is when the 5-year-old began chasing her.

The social workers then interviewed members of the Schlosser family as well as Dena, learning that Dena had been acting strangely for a while. According to her family members, Dena often appeared withdrawn and depressed, and when she did talk, it was about strange things, such as the impending Apocalypse.

Because of all of these factors, John had Dena committed to a mental health facility for a few weeks. She was diagnosed with mental illness but was never determined to be violent or a threat to herself or others. "There was never any indication of violence with this family," said social worker Marissa Gonzalez. "The children had always been healthy, happy, and cared for."

She came back home, and through late 2004, it seemed as though she had turned the corner and would overcome her demons. But no matter how much medication one may take, problems as profound as Dena Schlosser's often have a way of working their way back to the surface.

"He Touched Me"

By the fall of 2004, Dena's condition had taken a drastic turn. She appeared to be living in another world of her own making and there was little that anyone did could bring her out of it. John thought that, since she was always such a devout Christian, that bringing her to church more would help, but it seemed to have the opposite effect.

The Schlossers belonged to the Water of Life Church outside of Dallas. It was one of many evangelical Christian churches in the area, but it had been growing tremendously in terms of members and profile in the years before 2004. A large reason why the church was growing, and why the Schlossers liked the church, was because of its charismatic preacher, Doyle Davidson.

Being an evangelical preacher in the "Bible Belt" is a lot harder than you may think. Since there is a lot of competition, to be a successful, long-term evangelical preacher in the south, one has to not only be charismatic but also know how to walk the thin line between fire and brimstone and motivation. A preacher will lose his flock if he is too negative, so the best Bible Belt preachers usually employ a positive message along with their threats of eternal damnation. Doyle Davidson was one such preacher.

Dena in particular was impressed with Davidson. She thought that the preacher was personally speaking to her when he discussed the book of Revelation and what it means for the future of the planet. Dena Schlosser began to believe that Doyle Davidson had the key to unlock the mysteries of the Apocalypse. She constantly looked for signs of the impending Apocalypse until she finally thought she found them during a news broadcast. When Dena heard a report about a boy getting mauled by a lion, for some reason, she believed that was a sure sign that the end times were just around the corner.

She had to do her part, which meant making sure the most innocent member of the Schlosser family didn't have to suffer. So, one day after church, Dena "offered" Margaret to Davidson, who refused the offer. For most people, such an offer would've led to commitment in a mental facility, but because Dena had been acting so bizarrely for so long, it just seemed to have been ignored.

But no one would be able to ignore what Dena did on the evening of November 22, 2004. John and the two older daughters were gone, leaving Dena alone with Margaret. It's unknown if she planned what she did, or if she just took the opportunity when she was alone with the baby, but she wasted little time.

Dena put on some gospel music and then committed one of the most unspeakable acts one could imagine. She didn't suffocate or stab to death her helpless daughter, which of course would've been terrible, but instead, she cut off Margaret's arms. Yes, you read that right, Dena cut off Margaret's little arms.

Using a kitchen knife, Dena did the diabolical act quickly as the loud gospel music drowned out the sounds of her daughter's cries. When she was done, Dena left the baby's arms in the crib and called 911. The confused 911 operator heard Dena say, "I cut off her arms" as the gospel song "He Touched Me" played loudly in the background.

The responding police officers were horrified by what they found. All of the first responders on the scene that day had seen plenty of death and violence in their careers but nothing that approached the level of what they saw in the Schlosser home that evening. It was either the evilest or most deranged thing they had ever witnessed. And that was the question that was immediately asked: was Dena Schlosser evil or insane?

The police arrested her for murder and the Collin County, Texas district attorney charged her with murder, believing she was in control of her faculties, but Dena's lawyers argued at trial that she was insane. To bolster their case, the defense attorneys pointed to Dena's bizarre behavior in the months before the murder and the fact that she had been briefly hospitalized.

Most in the Dallas area believed that there was no way a jury would not find Dena Schlosser guilty of murder. That is until the Andrea Yates retrial took place. Yates had her retrial for the murders of her children in the summer of 2006, and if you'll recall, she was found not guilty by reason of insanity. Schlosser's lawyers were hoping for a similar verdict just a few months later.

Among the evidence that Schlosser's lawyers presented to the jury were some scans that showed she had a brain tumor and expert testimony that she suffered from postpartum psychosis. The evidence for Schlosser's insanity was so convincing that even the prosecution experts seemed to agree with the assessment. "She felt she was basically commanded, in essence, to cut Maggie's arms off and her own arms off, and her legs and her head, and in some way to give them to God," said state psychiatrist David Self at the trial.

The trial ended in early November 2006 and on November 7, 2006, the jury came back with its verdict—not guilty by reason of insanity. It was the second time in less than six months that a Texas jury had returned a not guilty by reason of insanity jury for a notorious child-killing mom. The verdict upset a large part of the community and caused divisions among neighbors and coworkers—although the majority of the public opposed the verdict, a significant minority believed that Dena truly was insane.

And for those who believed that Dena Schlosser should be punished for her heinous act, the road she faced was neither easy nor enjoyable. Although Dena Schlosser was found not criminally guilty or liable for her daughter's murder, it was because she was insane, which meant that she automatically became a ward of the state. Like Andrea Yates months earlier, Schlosser was committed to a mental hospital for an indeterminate period. Not long after the trial, Dena was sent to the North Texas State Hospital in Vernon, Texas. Dena Schlosser will never have complete freedom or so most people thought.

Dena and Andrea

When Dena was sent to the mental hospital, it was far from the end of her story. When Dena Schlosser was found not guilty by reason of insanity, it just began a new chapter in a very strange book.

Not long after Dena was sent away, John filed for divorce and full custody of the couple's two surviving children. He had no plans to stand by Dena during her long-term treatment. No one blames John for moving on either. He did believe that she needed treatment instead of prison, but there was no way he could stay with her. Every time he looked at Dena, he was reminded of his baby's agonizing death and the final few moments of life as she struggled in the crib. The Schlosser's two daughters have also ended all contact with their mother.

So, Dena was sent to the hospital to begin her treatment that could last a lifetime, but she wasn't going to go through the treatment alone. When Dena was assigned a room, she learned that she had an equally notorious roommate, Andrea Yates. By all accounts, the two women got along and Dena adjusted quickly to her new living conditions. Andrea showed Dena the ropes of institutional living and the two shared similar, if not twisted, theological views of the world. Yates and Schlosser could often be seen reading the Bible together and discussing different verses from the Old and New Testaments. Both women seemed to particularly enjoy the fierier passages from the Old Testament.

Dena didn't give the staff at the hospital any problems and generally got along well with the other patients, although she was closest to Yates. She was put on a heavy medical regime of anti-psychotics and anti-depression pills and had regular group and individual therapy sessions. Overall, Dena responded well to everything and when she came up for review in late 2008, her doctors only had positive things to say.

According to the doctors of the North Texas State Hospital, Dena Schlosser was no longer a threat to herself or others. Under the terms of her confinement, if Schlosser was no longer deemed to be a threat, she could be released back into society. So, in November 2008, exactly two years after she was determined to be not guilty by reason of insanity, Dena Schlosser was released from custody. Since she wasn't a convicted criminal, Dena's release wasn't public record. Therefore, no one outside of the staff at the hospital knew she had been released.

The conditions of Schlosser's release were pretty stringent, though. She was essentially under house arrest and only allowed to leave her

146

apartment for work, church, or therapy. She was also barred from being around children. Still, it was pretty incredible that she was allowed to walk among the rest of us when one considers her crime. To have a level of anonymity and also presumably for safety reasons, Dena legally changed her last name back to her maiden name.

Despite being released back onto the streets, the reality is that Dena Schlosser/Laettner is a very disturbed individual. Just over a year after being released from the state hospital, in April 2010, Dena was picked up for wandering around the Dallas suburb of Richardson, Texas in the early morning hours. Neighbors of the quiet community called the police when they noticed the strange woman walking back and forth down the street, apparently talking to herself. The responding police officers initially weren't able to determine much because she kept babbling to herself, but after a while, they learned that she had previously been committed to a mental hospital.

Dena was briefly recommitted to a hospital after the incident. Dena was then released under the same conditions as her first release. She kept a low profile in the Dallas area and landed a low-paying job at Walmart under her maiden name. But in today's society, where everything is posted online and people have access to virtually all records, nothing can be completely private. Someone found out that Dena was working at a Dallas area Walmart, and before too long, the story became viral and was picked up by local news outlets.

The managers of the local Walmart faced intense scrutiny, though, in fairness to them, Dena applied for the job under her maiden name and technically had no criminal record. Still, the pressure was too much so they fired the murdering mom from the job. Dena Laettner hasn't been heard of since, so one can only think where she is now. She could be living next door to you!

CHAPTER 16

PROTECTING HER TERRITORY, JESSICA EDENS

Men may be statistically more violent than women, but as this book shows, there are more than a few women out there who like to challenge that fact. Most historians, anthropologists, and biologists state that the reason men are more violent is a product of a combination of nature, evolution, and circumstances. In the Paleolithic Era, the men who survived and reproduced were the ones who were usually the most violent: they could effectively protect their women, children, and tribe.

This continued into historic times and was replicated on a larger scale, with kingdoms fighting over resources, which at times included women. The idea of men fighting over "territory," which can include wives or girlfriends, is still seen today. You've no doubt seen this behavior somewhere in your lifetime, often at a bar where alcohol is involved, and although most of us today try to avoid this type of behavior, the origins of it are still deep inside most men.

You've probably heard it called the "caveman instinct," and although it is primarily associated with men, it can also be seen in women at times. Women in the Paleolithic Era also had to compete for resources and a strong male protector. The women who could win the best male protector were usually the best looking, smartest, and most fertile women in the tribe. This primitive instinct to attract the ablest man, many believed, still also exists deep inside most women and is what makes some women very territorial. Almost as territorial as men.

Unfortunately, some people—men and women—are unable to control their primitive impulse to assert their territoriality. They fail to realize that we live in a civilized society and that, in return for all of the comforts we get to enjoy, we must relinquish some of our primitive urges.

The final case in this anthology is about a wife and mother named Jessica Edens who learned that another woman had moved in on her territory. Instead of realizing that it was time to move on with her life and that there was little she could do, Jessica decided that not only would her sexual competitor pay for the invasion of territory, but also everyone around her would as well. This left her husband with nothing and wondering if he could have done things differently.

Ben and Jessica Edens

Ben and Jessica Edens met in the late 2010s in Greenville, South Carolina. Both had good jobs when they met and hit it off well. Jessica liked Ben a lot—he was good looking, successful, and charming—but she worried that her son Hayden from a previous marriage would be a deal-breaker.

It turned out that Ben and Hayden really liked each other, and most importantly, Ben showed an interest in being a father figure. The situation made Jessica ecstatic since she didn't get along with her ex-husband, who had minimal contact with Hayden. After a whirlwind courtship, Ben proposed to Jessica and she readily accepted. The two moved into a nice, new home in a quiet suburban neighborhood and began to build a life together.

Things went well for the couple in the first few years. They welcomed daughter Harper to their family in 2012, there was plenty of money coming into the home, and Ben was a good father to Hayden. But as most couples do, in 2015 and 2016, the Edens hit a couple of rough patches. Things began with arguments over domestic duties and occasional fights over finances. Of course, these are pretty common in families today, even in those that don't have any financial problems. The arguments started to take on a more accusatorial tone from Jessica. She became more possessive of Ben, staking out her "territory."

If you've ever personally experienced a possessive person, then you know that things don't usually end well for them. You just can't "claim your territory" over another human today like you could in the Paleolithic Era—doing so will just drive the person away into someone else's arms. Yet Jessica persisted with her possessive nature, nagging Ben by constantly asking where he was, where he was going, and calling him incessantly.

Needless to say, Ben didn't react well to the possessive behavior and would argue with her, which often led to loud, blow-out arguments in front of the children. By 2015, Ben primarily slept on the couch and the love had gone out of their marriage. Since Ben was young, successful, and good looking, he caught the eyes of other women. One woman who caught his eye was a 27-year-old who he met at work in 2016 named Meredith Rahme. She was attractive, young, and had no children. Most importantly, Rahme didn't try to control Ben's every move.

Not long after meeting, Ben and Meredith began a sexual affair that quickly became something more. Ben fell in love with Meredith and planned to marry her, but of course, he was still married to Jessica, so he had to break the news to her. She didn't take the news very well.

Jessica tried to shame Ben for having a lack of morals and when that didn't work, she attempted to make him feel guilty for leaving the children. No matter how much guilt and shame Jessica tried to heap on Ben, though, he just became more determined to end the marriage. Ben moved out of the Edens home in April 2017 and into an apartment with Meredith Rahme.

Jessica was hurt by the deterioration of her marriage, but anger and hatred more accurately describe the emotions that were driving her at that point. Just like a mother bear protecting its family from outsiders, Jessica began focusing her wrath on the "homewrecker" Meredith Rahme. Jessica made several unflattering posts about Meredith on social media, and when that didn't seem to have much of an effect, she went right to the source by sending her text messages.

Meredith felt threatened by the text messages, so she reported them to the local police on July 12, 2017. The police then visited Jessica. The attractive Jessica acted demure when the police arrived at her home and made the entire incident appear to be a misunderstanding. Jessica admitted that she and Ben were having marriage problems and that Meredith Rahme was a part of the problem, but that she didn't blame Meredith.

She assured the officers that she wasn't a violent person and that she would never do anything that could jeopardize her children. Although the responding officers could've arrested Jessica on a terroristic threat charge, they found the mother convincing. They believed that it was a combination of a little bit of anger and some major misunderstandings and that everything would probably be cleared up the next day between the involved parties. The cops were right, everything would be cleared up the next day, but everyone involved would be dead!

"Everyone You Love Is Gone"

After the police left the Edens home, Jessica knew that she wasn't going to win the fight without having to shed blood. Jessica cleaned and polished the .40 caliber pistol she took from her parents' home. She didn't want it jamming when she carried out her plan. It would be a big day for Jessica because it would be the day when she marked her territory once and for all. And Jessica knew that she would only have one chance to carry out her plan.

After cleaning the gun, she buckled Hayden and Harper into their car seats. The two children didn't think anything was out of the ordinary, and by all accounts, Jessica just let them think that they were going on just another trip around town. The first stop was Meredith Rahme's apartment.

Jessica waited outside of the apartment awhile for Meredith. It was still relatively early, so when Meredith came outside to her car, she was still probably waking up and more concerned about getting to work on time than what was waiting for her around the corner. It only took one shot to finish Meredith off.

Jessica viewed her handiwork for a few moments. She knew that she had crossed the Rubicon at this point and there was no going back. Jessica had killed her rival, but there was no way she was going to spend the rest of her life behind bars. Jessica had to go through with the next, toughest part of her plan.

It remains unknown if the children saw their mother murder Rahme. It doesn't matter, though, because after killing her, Jessica drove a few miles down Interstate 85, pulled over, and shot each of Hayden and Harper one time in the head. Jessica then made a disturbing call to Ben. "Everyone you love is gone," screamed Jessica into the phone. "Do you hear me? I'm about to be gone too." Then there was the sound of a gunshot.

In the days following Jessica's massacre, friends and family of the couple were left searching for answers. There, of course, was the standard, "I should have seen the signs" statements by some who were close to Jessica, but the reality is that there would've been no way to stop what she did. Jessica was driven by an urge to protect what was hers, taken to an extreme level, combined with a twisted sense of honor, and a strong desire for revenge.

The reality is that Jessica kept her true feelings close to her heart. She let very few people know what she was thinking and feeling. A search of the Edens home revealed that Jessica's massacre had been planned well before the actual murders, as evidenced by several letters she wrote to those closest to her. In a letter addressed to her parents, Jessica told them how much she loved them and that she was truly sorry for bringing them shame and killing their grandchildren.

She also wrote a letter to her ex-husband and the father of Hayden: "To Nate, I don't know what to say. You gave me my first child. I will forever be grateful because of you. I never meant to cause you so much pain as this, I am sorry."

But for Ben, she wrote her longest and most searing letter: "To Ben, You have caused me more pain that I've ever been in my life. You have caused my children pain. i hate you. I hope you rot one day for what you have done to me and my kid. You can no longer hurt us, We are at peace. Hope you live with pain and shame and guilt for the rest of your life."

The massacre has left Ben Edens emotionally shattered, although unlike Jessica would've liked to have believed, it probably didn't make him question how he treated her, just why he didn't leave her earlier. Or that he had never met her in the first place.

CONCLUSION

So, there you have it, without doubt, 16 of the worst mothers in American history. Some killed their children out of a twisted type of revenge, while others did so for profit. Some of these killer moms seemed to enjoy murder but for others, it was just a means to an end. Some of these women are legally insane, one was more irresponsible than anything, and many of them are pure evil.

Chances are, if you're reading this, even if you've had problems with your mother, she doesn't even come close to what you've seen here. These women are certainly a small minority of all mothers, but as the cases covered women from nearly every race, economic background, and different regions of the country, it demonstrates that the phenomenon of mothers who kill their own is unfortunately a little more common than we would like to think.

Nearly everyone who knew the killer moms in this book was surprised when they learned the news that their friend, neighbor, or family members had killed her children. Either they ignored the warning signs or there were none. The sad reality is that cases like these are almost impossible to prevent or predict.

Sure, people always say "I should have known," after the fact, but no one ever thinks that a mother will massacre her entire family. A part of that is because most of us don't want to see the worst in people. Even if we see some signs that something is wrong, there is no way that we would ever think that a mother could take the step of killing her entire family.

Because a mother who murders her children is perhaps the most difficult crime to understand.

MORE BOOKS BY JACK ROSEWOOD

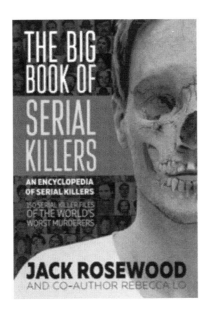

There is little more terrifying than those who hunt, stalk and snatch their prey under the cloak of darkness. These hunters search not for animals, but for the touch, taste, and empowerment of human flesh. They are cannibals, vampires and monsters, and they walk among us.

These serial killers are not mythical beasts with horns and shaggy hair. They are people living among society, going about their day to day activities until nightfall. They are the Dennis Rader's, the fathers, husbands, church going members of the community.

This A-Z encyclopedia of 150 serial killers is the ideal reference book. Included are the most famous true crime serial killers, like Jeffrey Dahmer, John Wayne Gacy, and Richard Ramirez, and not to mention the women who kill, such as Aileen Wuornos and Martha Rendell. There are also lesser known serial killers, covering many countries around the world, so the range is broad.

Each of the serial killer files includes information on when and how they killed the victims, the background of each killer, or the suspects in some cases such as the Zodiac killer, their trials and punishments. For some there are chilling quotes by the killers themselves. The Big Book of Serial Killers is an easy to follow collection of information on the world's most heinous murderers.

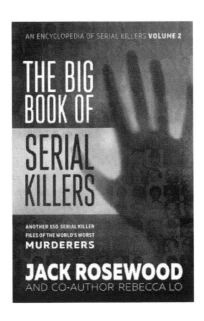

Our first volume caused such an impact that we've decided to bring you the long-awaited Volume 2 of the most comprehensive Serial Killer encyclopedia ever published!

Murderers or monsters, normal people turned bad or people born with the desire to kill; it doesn't matter where they come from, serial killers strike dread into our hearts with a single mention of their names. Hunting in broad daylight or stalking from the shadows, we are their prey and their hunt is never done until they are caught or killed.

With a worrying number of them living in our communities, working alongside us at our places of employment and sharing the same spaces where we spend time with our families, serial killers are typically just another neighbor that we barely think about. A worrying thought, to be honest.

In The Big Book of Serial Killers Volume 2 we go through the lives of 150 serial killers who allowed themselves to fall under the influence of their darkest desires and took the lives anywhere from one to one hundred victims; we speak of their motives and how their stories ended (*if* they ended...), and remind you of the fear and pain that they left behind.

But what can you expect from **The Big Book of Serial Killers Volume 2?**

You will find such things as:

- An excellent A-Z list of all of these deadly killers, allowing you to reference the encyclopedia whenever you need to find out more about any single murderer.
- All of the uncensored details of their crimes, with much effort taking into account to describe their horrific acts.
- Important information on their date and place of birth, date of arrest and number of victims, among other facts.
- A list of Trivia facts for each killer, allowing you to learn more about their personalities and any films or documentaries made about them.

So, with nothing more to add – it's only time now for you purchase this book and begin learning about 150 of the sickest, most dangerous serial killers in world history.

This is the next level in murder: are you ready to learn about the evilest men and women in history?

Made in the USA
Columbia, SC
25 March 2022